LARGE PI...

Crossword Puzzle Book for Adults

Volume 1

For more fun puzzle books
visit our Amazon store!

For US Puzzlers: bit.ly/rosenbladt
For UK Puzzlers: bit.ly/rosenbladt-uk
For CA Puzzlers: bit.ly/rosenbladt-ca

ACROSS
1. Listen attentively
5. Quick
10. Agave
14. Tennis star, - Natase
15. Ammonia derivative
16. Genuine
17. Vanishing
19. Face cover
20. Lacking salt
21. Card game for two
23. Vase
24. "Beauty ___ the eye ..."
25. Crazy
27. Held
32. Covered with bark
33. Gluck's "___ ed Euridice"
34. Nigerian native
35. Actress Judith
36. Nickel-cadmium battery
37. A particular
38. "Gloria in excelsis ___"
39. Fragrant flower
40. Alpine river
41. Student's worry
43. Classify
44. Flock of cattle
45. Gear wheel
46. Melodic
49. Zigged and zagged
54. Restaurateur Toots
55. Enthusiasm
57. Writing implements
58. Related maternally
59. Garage sale warning
60. Ed.'s request
61. Observant one
62. To a smaller extent

DOWN
1. Hastens
2. Edison's middle name
3. Monetary unit of Iran
4. U.S. State
5. Ascended
6. Gremlins, Pacers, etc.
7. Pastry items
8. Tavern
9. Hated
10. Big name in fashion
11. "Laughable Lyrics" writer
12. Kiln for drying hops
13. Actress Sommer
18. N.F.L. Hall-of-Famer Hirsch
22. Goodbye
24. Actually
25. Washes
26. Nabisco cookies
27. Convoluted
28. Killer whales
29. Saltpeter
30. "I Hated, Hated, Hated This Movie" author
31. Cupola
32. Wait
36. Common gas
37. Equiangular
39. Cleaning cabinet supplies
40. Capri, e.g.
42. On horseback
45. Antic
46. Egyptian serpents
47. Ostrichlike bird
48. Charged particles
49. "Now!"
50. Stringed instrument
51. Inventory: Abbr.
52. Auspices: Var.
53. Make temporary sleeping place (Colloq)
56. "Another Green World" composer

Puzzle 2

ACROSS

1. 1930's boxing champ Max
5. Ancient city NW of Carthage
10. "___ boy!"
14. Sicilian city
15. "The Age of Bronze" sculptor
16. Food
17. Break down into harmless products
19. Yield
20. Invigorates
21. Flips
23. Morose
24. Prepare patient for operation
25. Boatswain
27. Argillite
32. Utah lilies
33. Lariat
34. Dorm overseers, for short
35. "Put ___ writing"
36. Earthquake
37. Datum
38. Dallas cager, briefly
39. Cremona artisan
40. The writer Saki's real name
41. Pen-name
43. "Bus Stop" playwright
44. Places
45. S.A.S.E., e.g.
46. Fermented soybean cake
49. Province in central Canada
54. Adriatic port
55. Thrifty
57. "No returns"
58. Mysterious
59. Roman emperor after Galba
60. 20th letter of the Hebrew alphabet
61. Splash through mud
62. Political cartoonist called "our best recruiting sergeant" by Lincoln

DOWN

1. Tony winner Neuwirth
2. Has ___ with
3. Carbon compound
4. Hotel chain
5. Exhorted
6. Ripped
7. Argonaut who slew Castor
8. Spanish hero
9. Arterial dilatation
10. Receive
11. At that time
12. Mary in the White House
13. Inspires dread
18. Editor Harold
22. Mexican currency
24. Here and there
25. Greek letters
26. Pointed arch
27. Washes
28. Non-clergy
29. Big ape
30. Mother-of-pearl
31. "___ Perpetua" (Idaho's motto)
32. Fool
36. Overwhelms
37. Operate
39. Together, in music
40. Musical note
42. Uppity
45. Methuselah's father
46. Type of automatic gear selector (1-3)
47. Relax
48. Dr.'s orders
49. Prefix, one
50. Cuckoos
51. Prefix, eight
52. Scornful cries
53. "Thanks ___!"
56. ___-de-sac

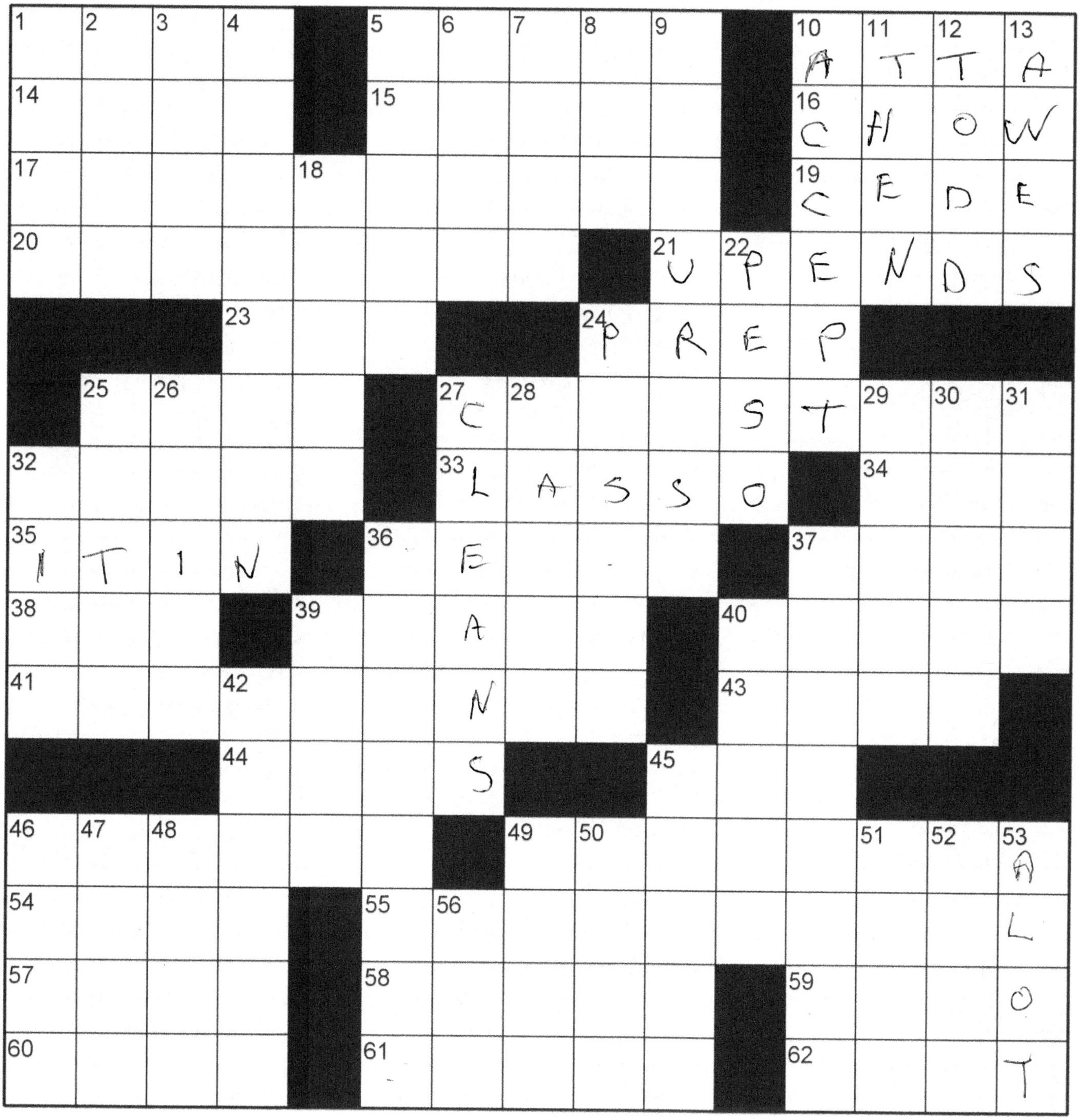

Puzzle 3

ACROSS
1. Clasp
5. Upturned, as a box
10. Certain NCO's
14. Long period of time
15. Mrs. Eisenhower
16. Weight allowance
17. Gods
19. Don Juan, e.g.
20. A lift
21. Looped
23. Printer's measures
24. Additional job benefit
25. Inventor Elias
27. Protestant of Northern Ireland
32. Flip out
33. Noisy
34. Clark's "Mogambo" co-star
35. Manhattan Project scientist
36. ___ Ababa
37. Growl
38. "No ___"
39. Sap
40. Labor leader George
41. The way of a sailor
43. Current month

44. 1984 World Series MVP Trammell
45. Airport abbr.
46. Heavy load
49. Recants
54. Sewing case
55. Pertaining to the earth's internal heat
57. ___ Fein
58. Overjoy
59. Breakwater
60. Cassini of fashion
61. Arabian currency
62. "Idylls of the King" character

DOWN
1. Jekyll's alter ego
2. Eye, at the Eiffel Tower
3. Wash
4. Vehicular access to property
5. Excludes
6. Western pact
7. Islamic chieftain
8. Never, in Neuss
9. Comes down
10. Hit
11. Jail
12. Genuine
13. Pip
18. Christened

22. Wild revelry
24. Striking ground with foot
25. Equine
26. Greek letter
27. Confer holy orders upon
28. "The Gates of Hell" sculptor
29. Supernatural powers
30. ___-garde
31. Never
32. Mouth parts
36. Organised
37. Police officer
39. Valley
40. Bishop's headdress
42. Losing colour
45. An anaesthetic
46. "Eso ___" (Paul Anka hit)
47. Gas, e.g.: Abbr.
48. Mysterious symbol
49. Brown and white horse
50. Blues singer James
51. "Follow me!"
52. Anklebones
53. Toboggan
56. Biblical high priest

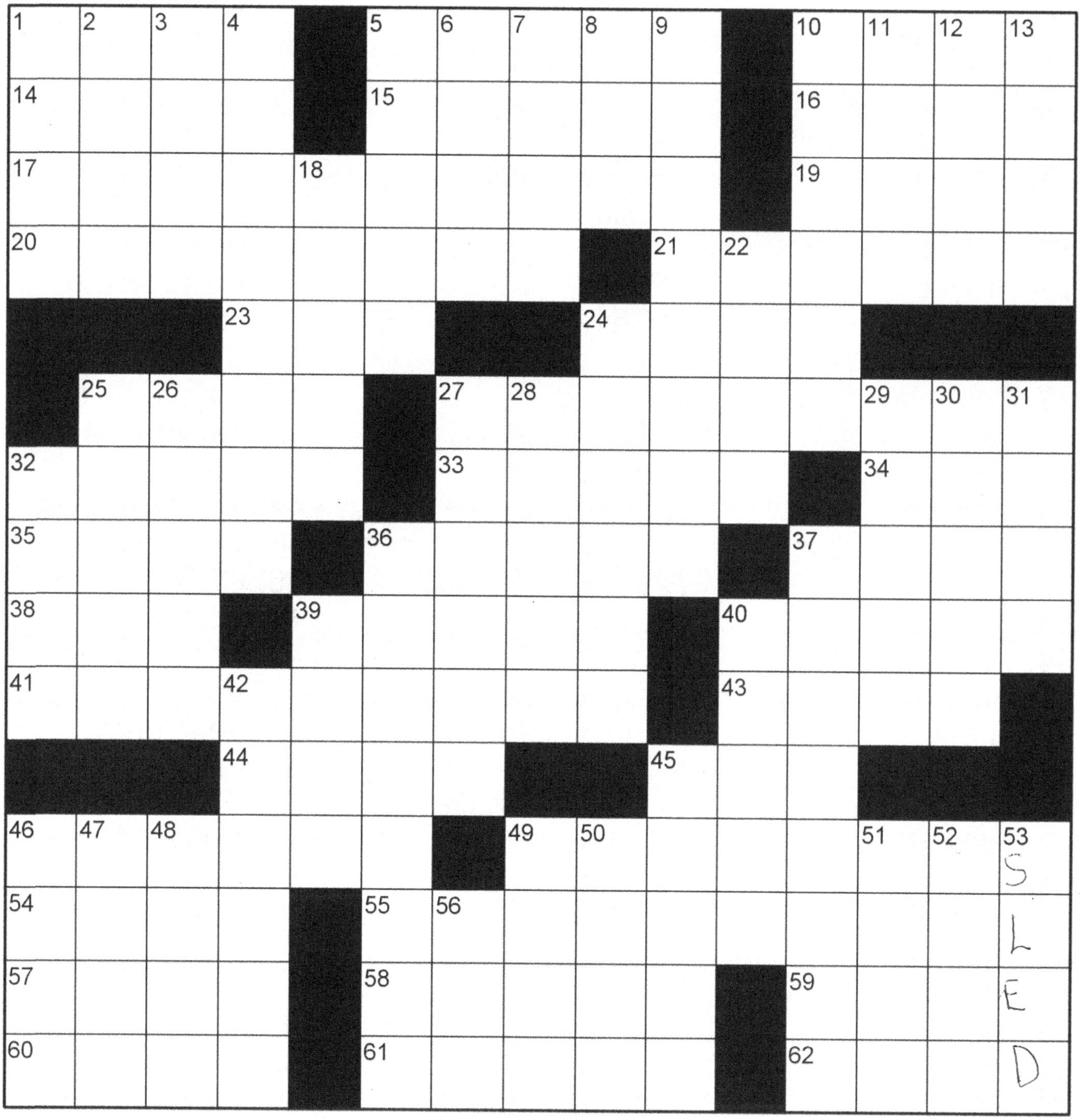
1 2 3 4 5 6 7 8 9 10 11 12 13
14 15 16
17 18 19
20 21 22
23 24
25 26 27 28 29 30 31
32 33 34
35 36 37
38 39 40
41 42 43
44 45
46 47 48 49 50 51 52 53
54 55 56
57 58 59
60 61 62
S
L
E
D

Puzzle 4

ACROSS

1. Tasks
5. Gumbo vegetables
10. Harvest
14. Rat-___
15. "The Old Wives' Tale" playwright
16. "Enchanted" girl in a 2004 film
17. Expert on bugs
19. Prayer
20. Plot outline
21. Bully, often
23. Columbus Day mo.
24. Mil. addresses
25. Mont. neighbor
27. Verbally stress
32. Life of ___
33. ___ lazuli
34. Classified abbr.
35. Had too much, briefly
36. Seraglio
37. Gardner and others
38. Decade
39. A craze
40. An instant
41. Glandular
43. Tier
44. Blows it
45. Photo
46. As a whole
49. Aphorism
54. Fannie ___ (securities)
55. Without friends
57. "Comin' ___ the Rye"
58. Wearies
59. Taverns
60. To bless
61. Escarpment
62. An appointment

DOWN

1. Chins
2. Auricular
3. Naked
4. Abnormally narrowed
5. Eyeball benders
6. French military cap
7. Bank take-back
8. Beer
9. Angels
10. Overtake again
11. Old cloth measures
12. To the sheltered side
13. Author of "I Kid You Not"
18. Sticky
22. Large snakes
24. Plea
25. One -, prejudiced
26. Coeur d'___, Idaho
27. African antelopes
28. Lunar "seas"
29. Monte ___ of Cooperstown
30. Hit
31. "___ quam videri" (North Carolina's motto)
32. Roster
36. Visits to the barber
37. Spider
39. 1960's-70's Italian P.M.
40. Banal
42. Trafalgar hero
45. Equilibrium
46. CPR pros
47. Okinawa port
48. When repeated, a vitamin B deficiency
49. Frizzy hair style
50. Preparatory school
51. Dame - Everage, Humphries' character
52. A man
53. Gds.
56. Zero

Puzzle 5

ACROSS
1. Moment
5. Protestant denom.
10. Glass bottle
14. Notion
15. The duck in "Peter and the Wolf"
16. A Great Lake
17. Gerontology
19. Fiddling Roman emperor
20. Having intelligence
21. Concealed
23. "48___"
24. Tony winner Neuwirth
25. Prevalent
27. Servility
32. Fake
33. Authentic
34. Aged
35. Tug
36. African republic
37. Tilled
38. Ear: Prefix
39. Death in Venice
40. Hungarian wine
41. Gullet
43. Org.
44. Just passable (2-2)
45. Person in a mask
46. Enclose in a sac
49. Listening part of a telephone receiver
54. Artist Chagall
55. Disinfection with fumes
57. American state
58. City near Venice
59. "Giovanna d'___" (Verdi opera)
60. A few
61. Waterlily
62. Grasslands

DOWN
1. Lively dances
2. ___ fixe
3. Fronded plant
4. Loyal
5. ___ Park, Colo.
6. Pornography (Colloq)
7. "What's ___ for me?"
8. Order to attack, with "on"
9. Redeemed
10. Person to whom a thing is sold
11. Angered
12. Frigid finish
13. Boxer Spinks
18. Buenos ___
22. Bibliographical abbr.
24. Contradicts
25. Disorderly flights
26. Eskimo dwelling
27. Exceed
28. African tribe
29. Cosy corners
30. Wash
31. Whirlpool
32. Fraternal gp.
36. Thrasonical
37. Sanatorium
39. Electrical units
40. Buccaneers' home
42. Human mind
45. Incites
46. Flightless flock
47. Western pact
48. Pack fully
49. Send out
50. Hokkaido native
51. Ireland
52. ___-Cola
53. "The Dukes of Hazzard" spinoff
56. Japanese vegetable

Puzzle 5

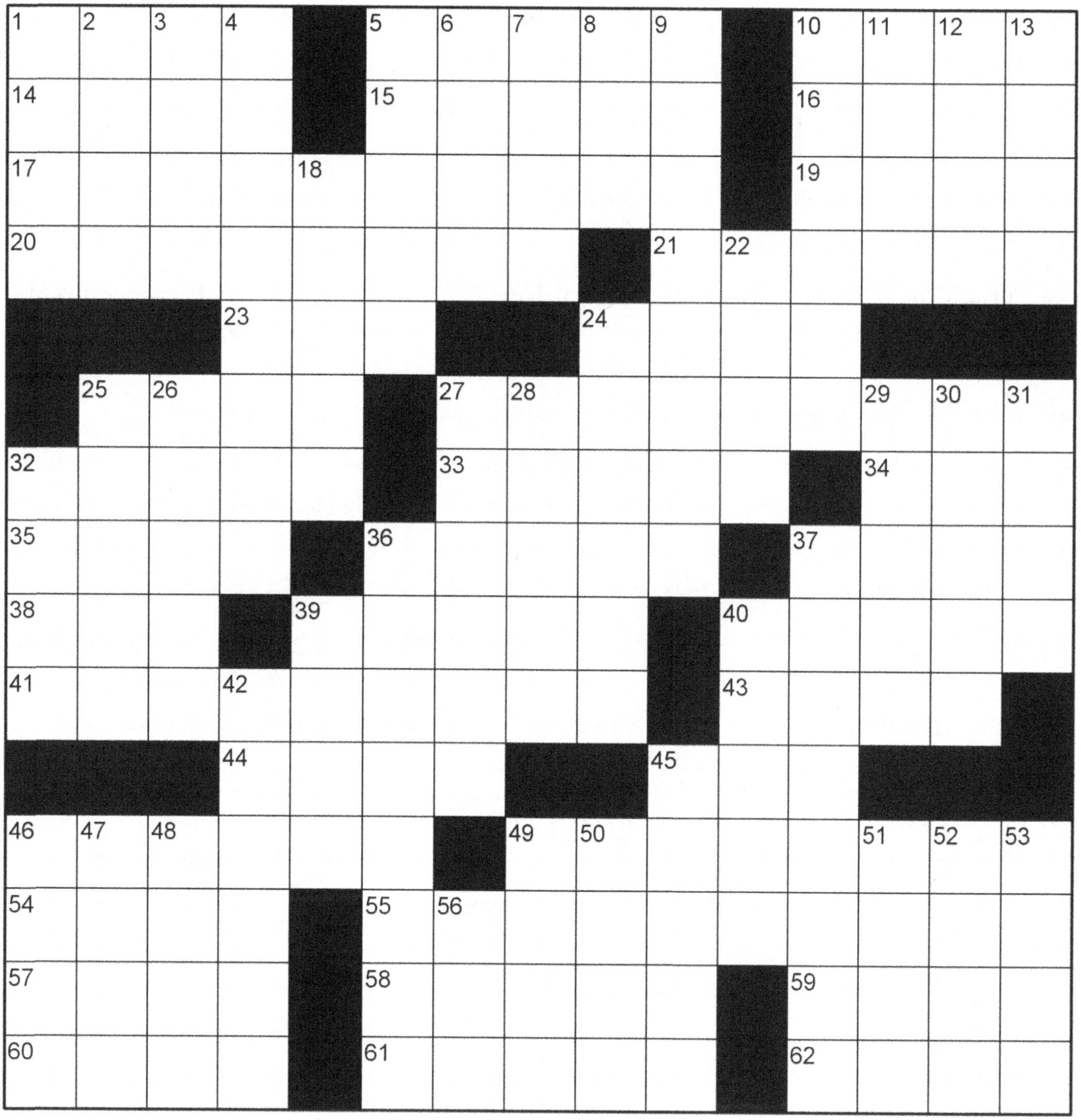

Puzzle 6

ACROSS

1. Boxing contest
5. Slews
10. Shoo
14. Stand
15. Eskimo dwelling
16. Dresden's river
17. Enormous
19. Black, as la nuit
20. Tidy state
21. Footnote word
23. They, in Tours
24. Polynesian root food
25. Final Four org.
27. Philistine
32. Cartoonist Trudeau
33. "Die Fledermaus" maid
34. Brassiere
35. "Comme ci, comme ça"
36. Suborn
37. Actress Taylor
38. Scottish hill
39. Dizzy
40. Filbert
41. Zealous advocate of an ideology
43. "Chestnuts roasting ___ open fire"
44. Wings
45. Conclusion
46. Group of four
49. Inhabitant of Sodom
54. K-12, in education
55. Wagon maker
57. Related
58. Counters
59. Proper word
60. Big ape
61. Arab country
62. Mother of the Valkyries

DOWN

1. Grain husk
2. Beauvais's department
3. Court grp.
4. Third
5. Climbing plants
6. Personalities
7. "Desire Under the ___"
8. "Vive le ___!"
9. Companionable
10. Oldest
11. Lump of clay
12. "___ Baby" ("Hair" song)
13. Expression
18. It's a relief
22. Highlands hillside
24. Triple
25. Unclothed
26. Davit
27. Sheer fabric
28. Farewell
29. Mediterranean tourist destination
30. "I Love a Parade" composer
31. Metal spike
32. Mongolian desert
36. Major avenue in New York City
37. Anti-personnel explosive
39. "It was ___ mistake!"
40. High public esteem
42. Rowing
45. Astronomer Hubble
46. Timber tree
47. Nevada city
48. Skinny
49. Thailand
50. At one time
51. Borodin's "Prince ___"
52. Dull sound
53. Sicilian volcano
56. "How to Succeed in Business Without Really Trying" librettist Burrows

13

ACROSS
1. Tins
5. Representative
10. Gall
14. Wreck
15. Shout of exultation
16. Cambridge colleges, for short
17. Study of urban problems
19. Soyuz rocket letters
20. Wind coming from the east
21. German cathedral city
23. Is able to
24. Hip bones
25. Essen basin
27. Minute blood vessel
32. Gowns
33. "Don't make ___!"
34. Inc., overseas
35. Head covering
36. Moon age at start of year
37. M.D.
38. Greek letter
39. "West Side Story" girl
40. Weaned pig
41. Suffering from asthma

43. Pond
44. Swedish pop-group of the '70s
45. PC linkup
46. 1930's-50's actor J. ___ Naish
49. Balanced
54. Command to horse
55. Changeable
57. New Mexico art community
58. Away
59. Ancient Peruvian
60. Concordes
61. Sleazy
62. Boardroom V.I.P.'s

DOWN
1. Rock's Motley ___
2. Subtle emanation
3. Person in authority
4. Grabbed
5. Rose prickle
6. Dixie pronoun
7. Ruse
8. Afr. nation
9. Someone who remains loyal
10. Pertaining to the cheek
11. Small measure
12. Adult nits

13. "Baseball Tonight" channel
18. Draws close to
22. Afflicts
24. Medicinal syrup
25. Origins
26. German submarine (1-4)
27. Per ___
28. Cremona craftsman
29. Allergy season sound
30. Monetary unit of Saudi Arabia
31. Recently: Abbr.
32. Ostrich-like bird
36. Making possible
37. Vocal
39. Early pulpit
40. Extends across
42. Torment
45. 1974 title role for Dustin Hoffman
46. 100-lb. units
47. Cries of discovery
48. Origin
49. Outer: Prefix
50. Empty
51. Norseman
52. Remarkable
53. Elhi orgs.
56. And not

Puzzle 8

ACROSS
1. Without
5. Rich tapestry
10. Mines
14. Indian bread
15. Indigent
16. Son of Isaac and Rebekah
17. Decorative
19. Capable
20. Made feeble
21. "How to Handle a Woman" lyricist
23. Superlative suffix
24. Old Chinese money
25. Public exhibition
27. Trunk of an elephant
32. Encore
33. Memento
34. Room within a harem
35. Geom. shape
36. Doctor
37. Wrongfully assist
38. Chi hrs.
39. Decaffeinated
40. Jazz singer Carmen
41. Formerly
43. Suffix with poet
44. Blunders
45. Malt beverage
46. Paste of inexpensive fish
49. Of mixed European and Asian parentage
54. At first: Abbr.
55. Recompense
57. Gist
58. Indian or Chinese
59. Auspices
60. Fast fleet
61. "Little" girl of old comics
62. Specks

DOWN
1. Frozen precipitation
2. River in central Switzerland
3. Grandmother
4. Dangerous place
5. Scottish, concerning
6. Mel's "Ransom" costar
7. Abbr. after many a general's name
8. Boise's county
9. Consisting of syllables
10. Oyster gems
11. Library ID
12. Story
13. Litigant
18. Quark-plus-antiquark particle
22. Fair-hiring org.
24. "L'chaim," literally
25. Excrete
26. Kind of knife
27. A summary
28. Barricade river again
29. Venomous snake
30. Perfect
31. Cloy
32. Medieval chest
36. Rhythmic
37. Got to
39. Suffix, skin
40. Where "Otello" premiered
42. Whinnies
45. Stadium
46. Absorbs, with "up"
47. "A God in Ruins" novelist
48. "Norma Rae" director
49. Send out
50. ___ the crack of dawn
51. The villain in Othello
52. Arguing
53. Scottish headland
56. Spanish bear

Puzzle 9

ACROSS

1. Whale herds
5. Italian composer
10. Surety
14. "Don't think so"
15. Pay for grazing
16. Wallaroo
17. Repository
19. 1982 Disney film
20. SA capital
21. Move, as a picture
23. Special attention, for short
24. Possess
25. Primates
27. Placoid
32. Author of "A Call to Service: My Vision for a Better America"
33. Split
34. Sicken
35. Oklahoma tribe
36. Donkeys
37. Nos. on checks
38. Compass heading
39. Arbor
40. "A Delicate Balance" playwright
41. Book of the New Testament
43. Amerada ___ (Fortune 500 company)
44. One having second thoughts
45. Exclamation of wonder
46. Least refined
49. A staff member
54. Score after deuce, in tennis
55. Blue
57. 1998 Wimbledon winner Novotna
58. Big name in stationery
59. Gael
60. Cathy ___, "East of Eden" wife
61. Children's doctor?
62. Relaxation

DOWN

1. Aqua ___
2. Expressed surprise
3. Dictator
4. Havens
5. Oracular
6. Minor oath
7. Staple Oriental grain
8. Cable alternative
9. Repeats
10. Sanctuary
11. Distinctive quality
12. Press clothes
13. Lengthy
18. Paralyze
22. Level
24. Nonsense
25. Insurance giant
26. Skulk
27. Hawkish
28. Compare
29. Poetic feet
30. Birds of prey
31. Otherwise
32. King ___
36. Halves
37. Tavern
39. Air conditioner capacity, for short
40. "Get ___ of yourself!"
42. Stadia
45. Unseals
46. Prince of India
47. First man
48. Grape beverage
49. "___, Brute!"
50. Electrical units
51. Pool site, maybe
52. Epic poetry
53. Punta del ___, Uruguay
56. Not

Puzzle 9

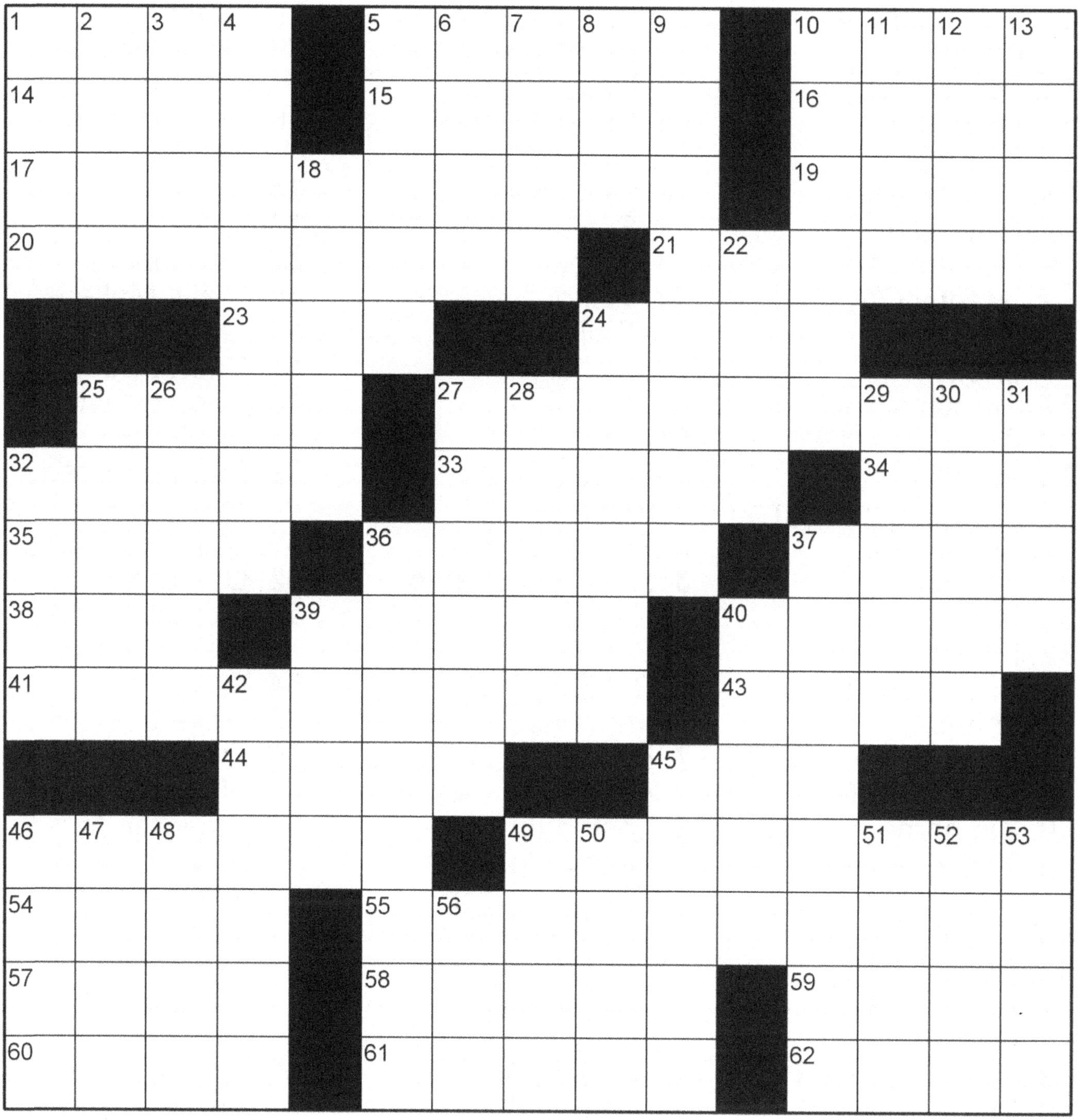

Puzzle 10

ACROSS
1. Ordeal
6. Cathedral
11. 1960's chess champ
14. Poets' feet
15. Deprive of courage
16. Where: Lat.
17. Greenish
19. Howard of "Happy Days"
20. Like a line, briefly
21. French story
22. Cosy
23. Wyatt -
25. Restless (music)
27. Symbol of success
31. Pitcher
32. Fuss
33. First name in hotels
35. Plains tribe
38. Actress Sofer
40. Big name in wine
42. Toni Morrison novel
43. A Gabor sister
45. Ditch
47. Art Ross Trophy org.
48. Medicinal plant
50. Threw caution to the wind
52. Run-down hotel
55. Fat
56. True
57. Hackneyed
59. Yours and mine
63. 10th letter of the Hebrew alphabet
64. Navy officer
66. Charlotte-to-Raleigh dir.
67. Consumed
68. Senior
69. Colour
70. Visitor
71. Children's doctor?

DOWN
1. Popular video recorder
2. Precipitation
3. Hungarian patriot Nagy
4. Bore
5. Bottle top
6. Impervious to dust
7. Donald Duck, to his nephews
8. Last letter of the Greek alphabet
9. Riding school
10. Hamilton's prov.
11. Reversal in circumstances
12. Around
13. Language
18. Weirder
22. Cancels a deletion
24. C.I.O.'s partner
26. W.W. II battle site, for short
27. Fairly hot
28. Notion
29. Farseeing or shrewd
30. Belgian painter James
34. Aide
36. K-12
37. Seasoning
39. "Let's Make ___"
41. Gave out
44. Short trader?
46. Supplement existence
49. Flat-bottomed rowboat
51. Star (Heraldry)
52. Dinner bird
53. Monetary unit of Sierra Leone
54. Rasp
58. Angers
60. Official language of Pakistan
61. Explorer John and others
62. Some cameras, for short
64. "Andy Capp" cartoonist Smythe
65. Criminal patterns, for short

Puzzle 10

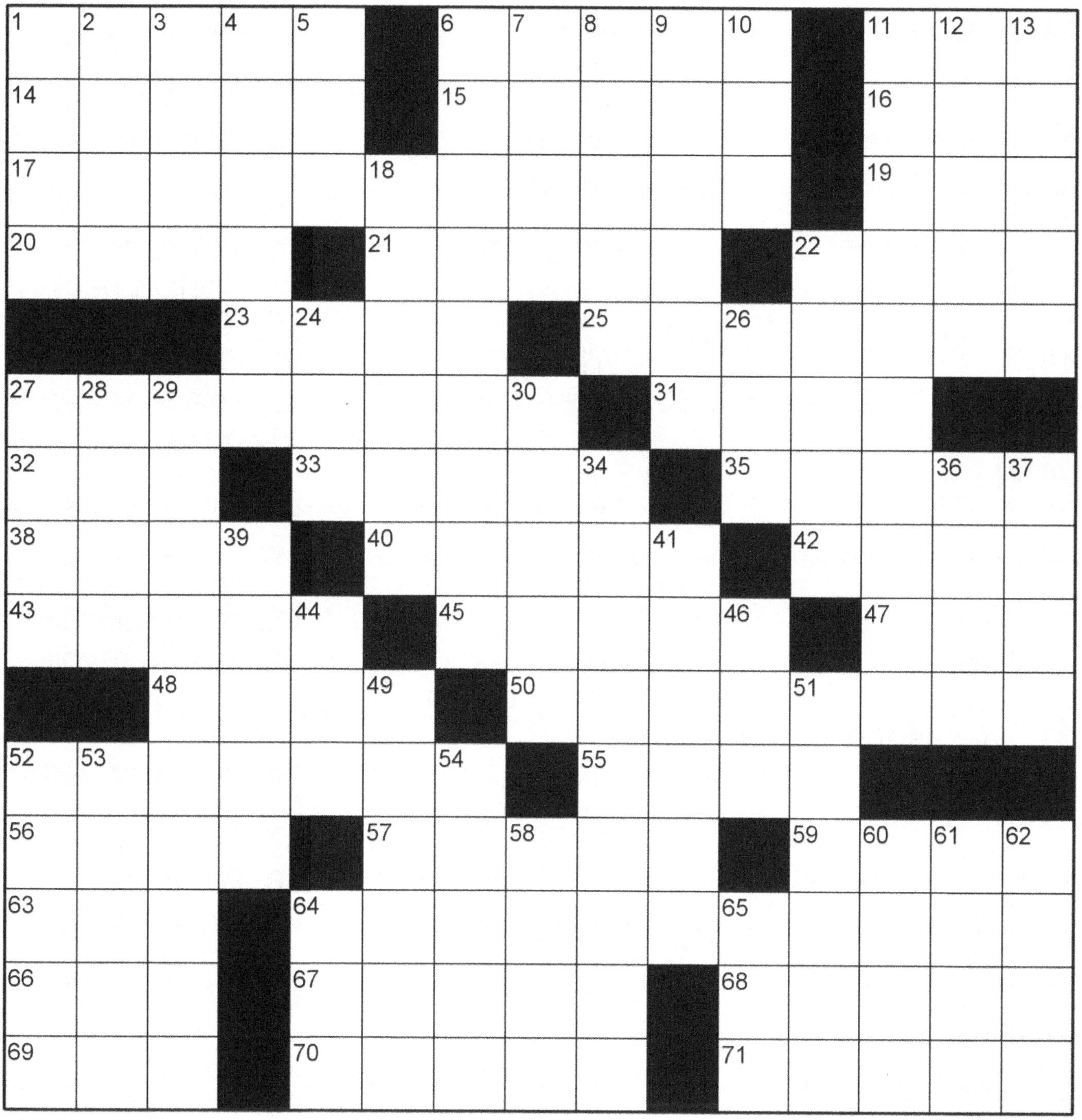

1 2 3 4 5 6 7 8 9 10 11 12 13
14 15 16
17 18 19
20 21 22
23 24 25 26
27 28 29 30 31
32 33 34 35 36 37
38 39 40 41 42
43 44 45 46 47
48 49 50 51
52 53 54 55
56 57 58 59 60 61 62
63 64 65
66 67 68
69 70 71

Puzzle 11

ACROSS

1. Small tree
6. Killer whales
11. IV amounts
14. Lean appearance
15. Stuffed savory vine leaf
16. Former measure of length
17. Grievous trouble
19. "___ won't be afraid" ("Stand by Me" lyric)
20. Not loco
21. Oily fruit
22. Breeding horse
23. Positions
25. Reflux of the tide
27. Suspect
31. Jack-in-the-pulpit, e.g.
32. Extrasensory perception
33. Suffix with Roman
35. Portents
38. Hebrew leader
40. Revolves
42. Egyptian deity
43. Transfer design
45. Downy duck
47. Antipollution org.
48. Ballet skirt
50. Fostered
52. Old-timer
55. Grate
56. Jiffs
57. Leather strip
59. Ostrich-like bird
63. 60's chess champ
64. Refusing to obey
66. Dined
67. "What ___!"
68. Letter-shaped opening
69. Radiation unit
70. "The Wreck of the Mary ___"
71. Vends

DOWN

1. Some N.C.O.'s
2. ___-kiri
3. Undoing
4. Unlatch door
5. A.C. letters
6. Female slave in a harem
7. French roast
8. Novelist Barker
9. Simple life form
10. Japanese word of respect
11. 1/100 of a meter
12. Cumulus
13. Slip
18. Grasshopper
22. Stub
24. Crude mineral
26. "My man!"
27. Honey liquor
28. Small island
29. Wearing spectacles
30. City on the Po
34. Tolerable
36. Back of neck
37. Certain herring
39. Woodland spirits
41. Shawl worn in Mexico
44. Inc., abroad
46. A.C.L.U. concerns: Abbr.
49. Upper portion
51. Rise in revolt
52. The Sun, for example
53. Gaucho's rope
54. Baffled
58. Lion's call
60. Hades
61. Chemical compound
62. Firm parts: Abbr.
64. Father
65. Cause of some shaking

Puzzle 12

ACROSS

1. Child's building cube
6. ___ New Guinea
11. Monetary unit of Vietnam
14. Iodine solution
15. Appliance brand
16. Fairy
17. Waking devices (5.6)
19. In the past
20. Enclosure with a MS.
21. Like some buckets
22. Spoken
23. Small animal
25. Gave to
27. Methane
31. Pastry item
32. Island (France)
33. Staid
35. Snicker
38. Gospel singer Winans
40. Peptic complaint
42. Minor oath
43. Skating jumps
45. Bibliographical abbr.
47. Food scrap
48. Strike breaker
50. Capable of being satiated
52. Dwells
55. "Shane" star
56. Among
57. Kenyan tribesman
59. Demonstration
63. Also
64. Without emotion
66. Sea eagle
67. Of a base
68. Disconnected
69. Fleur-de-___
70. Serpent
71. Russian emperors

DOWN

1. Prejudice
2. "Come Back, Little Sheba" wife
3. Harem rooms
4. Kitchen gadgets
5. Airline to Amsterdam
6. Agreeable to the taste
7. Crazily
8. Stepped
9. Disentangle
10. Small batteries
11. Sweetheart
12. Pond scum
13. Gone by
18. Black tea from China
22. Rowed
24. Sounds of hesitation
26. Singer, - "King" Cole
27. Flaky mineral
28. "Family Ties" role
29. Economic downturns
30. Cults
34. Able to be resold
36. Nobleman
37. Suffix, diminutive
39. Castilian hero
41. Opposite of wholesale
44. Sorrowful
46. Four times a day, in prescriptions
49. Bewail
51. Extras
52. Badger-like carnivore
53. Atlanta university
54. Chip dip
58. Badlands Natl. Park locale
60. Icelandic epic
61. Former Israeli P.M.
62. Chances
64. "60 Minutes" network
65. Not at home

24

Puzzle 13

ACROSS

1. "Otherwise..."
6. "Meet John Doe" director
11. 1957 Physics Nobelist Tsung-___ Lee
14. Crustaceans
15. Mountain nymph
16. Computer key
17. Ballet enthusiast
19. "Can't Help Lovin' ___ Man"
20. Film rating org.
21. Moon age at start of year
22. German "a"
23. Melody
25. Shrew
27. Skin emollient
31. Russian parliament before 1917
32. Prof.'s helpers
33. Ever
35. Trig function
38. "The Thin Man" canine
40. Blemish
42. Foot part
43. Recurring melody
45. Boredom
47. Fled
48. Unfeeling
50. Heavier-than-air craft
52. Error
55. "Happy Birthday, Moon" author

Frank
56. "I cannot tell ___"
57. High-toned
59. "Jake's Thing" author
63. Confederate soldier, for short
64. Thoughtful
66. Big picture?: Abbr.
67. Greek philosopher
68. Mixture of smoke and haze
69. Witness
70. Madison Avenue worker
71. University in Beaumont, Tex.

DOWN

1. Part of a nuclear arsenal, for short
2. Bind securely (Nautical)
3. "The Lion King" lion
4. Flattened at the poles
5. Canadian market inits.
6. Collaborate
7. First word of the "Aeneid"
8. Stone fruit
9. Raved
10. "The Sultan of Sulu" writer
11. Serving as a dedication
12. Yoga posture
13. Group of eight
18. Beliefs
22. St - fire (4'1)
24. Charlottesville sch.
26. Director Jean-___ Godard
27. Rat tail?
28. Whip
29. Pretended
30. "32 Flavors" singer Davis
34. Division into lines
36. 1984 World Series MVP Trammell
37. Hawaiian goose
39. Entertain
41. Nurtured
44. Invoice fig.
46. Games grp.
49. Observe
51. Teaching of the Buddha
52. Female horses
53. "Mr. Belvedere" actress Graff
54. ___ Games
58. Court grp.
60. Madam
61. Chichén ___ (Mayan city)
62. Prophet
64. Tax preparer, for short
65. Immigrant's class: Abbr.

27

Puzzle 14

ACROSS
1. Pet protection org.
6. Coronet
11. Shaker ___, O.
14. Biting
15. Bower
16. Conger
17. Uncontrolled
19. "The Simpsons" storekeeper
20. Certain NCO's
21. Bothered
22. American Indian
23. South American monkey
25. Earned
27. Study of human settlements
31. Dull
32. Criminal patterns, for short
33. Early computer
35. The New Yorker cartoonist Edward
38. Zeno's home
40. Cartoonist Wilson
42. Ward of "Sisters"
43. Incurred
45. Effort
47. Yellowfin tuna
48. ___ II (razor brand)
50. Skin of a deer
52. Voracious South American fish
55. Hip bones
56. Object of worship
57. Humiliate
59. Type of automatic gear selector (1-3)
63. Cut off
64. Stretchily
66. Biblical high priest
67. Prefix with linear
68. Serpent
69. U.S. Army medal
70. Impassive
71. Turkish generals

DOWN
1. Exclamations of surprise
2. Heroin
3. Saucy
4. Scabs
5. 1972 treaty subj.
6. Adept planner of tactics
7. Dies ___
8. The "A" in James A. Garfield
9. Utterly defeated
10. Limb
11. Great sorrow
12. Wigwam
13. Veered
18. Cloying
22. Slangy greetings
24. Manhattan addition
26. Four Monopoly properties: Abbr.
27. Like a 911 call: Abbr.
28. ___ nut
29. Having a constant entropy
30. Indian term of respect
34. Oversubtle
36. K-12
37. Reclined
39. Pertaining to the ear
41. Central parts
44. Kitchen utensil
46. Snow runner
49. Swiss cottage
51. Monetary unit of Thailand
52. Heaped
53. Objects of worship
54. Two islands in the N Bahamas
58. Italian wine province
60. Meaningless chatter
61. ___-Seltzer
62. Bakery selections
64. Bitter vetch
65. 11-member grp.

Puzzle 15

ACROSS

1. Cleft in two
6. Froths
11. Taxi
14. First
15. Suspension of breathing
16. Medical suffix
17. Painting executed in oil
19. Mothers
20. Salinger dedicatee
21. Mother-in-law of Ruth
22. Expectorate
23. Food regimen
25. "It's Too Late Now" autobiographer
27. Used in courts of law
31. The moon
32. Bullfight call
33. Academy Award
35. Small lizard
38. No longer working: Abbr.
40. Relaxed
42. - Connery
43. Gogol's "___ Bulba"
45. Free to attack
47. "Trust ___" (1937 hit)
48. "Betsy's Wedding" star
50. 1953 Kentucky Derby winner or a 1974 cult sci-fi film
52. Go over again
55. Knowing, as a secret
56. Ostentatious
57. Small yeast-raised pancake
59. Neighbor of Mo.
63. Kamoze of reggae
64. Planetary model
66. Monetary unit of Bulgaria
67. Race of Norse gods
68. Attentive
69. 180° from NNW
70. "Awake and Sing!" playwright
71. 1950's Ford flop

DOWN

1. Fraternal gp.
2. Eye part
3. Movie
4. Retard in movement
5. ___ 180
6. Rabid
7. Vision: Prefix
8. Soul
9. Servile
10. Droop
11. Unconcerned
12. Full speed
13. Moisten meat while cooking
18. Actually existing
22. Trig functions
24. Rescuer of Odysseus, in myth
26. Drinking vessel
27. Stronghold
28. Olive genus
29. Tending to retract
30. Looked over previous to robbing
34. Fees paid for services
36. ___ Sutra
37. Unique thing
39. Loiter
41. "Fiddlesticks!"
44. Star Wars, initially
46. Bout stopper, for short
49. Strolled
51. Slept noisily
52. Train tracks
53. Sea eagles
54. World-weary
58. "What's ___ for me?"
60. Relations
61. Stringed instrument
62. ___ nitrate
64. Kung ___ chicken
65. Consumed

Puzzle 16

ACROSS
1. Absorb
6. More secure
11. Special attention, for short
14. Porcelain
15. Make law
16. That woman
17. Render physically insensible
19. Brit. record label
20. Pierce with horn
21. Ancient Roman magistrate
22. Arrive
23. Dugout shelter
25. Had the aroma (of)
27. Sewerage outflow
31. Mars: Prefix
32. ___ Fail (Irish coronation stone)
33. Place
35. Indian melodies
38. "Ol' Man River" composer
40. Academy award
42. Wee
43. Erased
45. Cut
47. Cape ___, Mass.
48. Explorer called "the Red"

50. Constructive
52. Unconscious
55. US space agency
56. Basics
57. French fries
59. "Citizen ___"
63. Scale note
64. Abstainer from alcohol
66. - kwon do (Korean martial art)
67. Command
68. Terrors
69. Gonorrhea, e.g.: Abbr.
70. Cook in oven
71. Old "Hollywood Squares" regular

DOWN
1. Heroin
2. "___ you don't!"
3. Jetty
4. Open tomb or envelope
5. Dab
6. Shabbiness
7. Against
8. Flunks
9. Inflammatory condition of the skin
10. 66, e.g.: Abbr.
11. Person versed in theology
12. "I wanna!"

13. Bawled
18. To this
22. Wedge
24. Public transport
26. Go wrong
27. Nevada county
28. Fee
29. Improbable
30. Be silent
34. Type of sofa
36. Years abroad
37. Synchronize
39. ___ Circus (where St. Peter was crucified)
41. Cast again
44. "What's the ___?"
46. Football positions: Abbr.
49. "O tempora! O mores!" orator
51. U.S. sharpshooter
52. Kilns
53. German submarine
54. Silents star Bara
58. Residents: Suffix
60. Astronaut Bean
61. Dweeb
62. Gaelic
64. Rocky peak
65. Half of a 1955 merger: Abbr.

Puzzle 17

ACROSS
1. Aviates
6. Shallow water
11. Any insect
14. Decorated Murphy
15. Finnish architect Alvar ___
16. Biblical high priest
17. Heedless
19. Years, to Yves
20. ___-majeste
21. Blessing preceder
22. Move off hastily
23. Santa ___, Calif.
25. Calms
27. Most untidy
31. Naive person
32. Invoice abbr.
33. Unit of capacity
35. Wild
38. Heavy metal
40. Curtain fabric
42. A few
43. French city
45. Salsa singer Cruz
47. Ariz. neighbor
48. Censorship-fighting org.
50. Tenants collectively
52. Steep slopes
55. Rocky tableland
56. Obligation
57. Spartan serf
59. Big name in computer games
63. News initials
64. Streamlined
66. Prefix, whale
67. Wooden box
68. Evergreen tree
69. Amount past due?
70. Rhodes of Rhodesia
71. Small islands

DOWN
1. Flunk
2. Crescent-shaped figure
3. Writer Tarbell and others
4. Downy ducks
5. A few: Abbr.
6. Given to the use of sarcasm
7. Obsolete form of has
8. Bread spreads
9. When there's darkness, in a Koestler title
10. Auction item
11. Adjacent to a beach
12. Arm bones
13. Central points
18. Enter cautiously
22. Eye sores
24. Lubricant
26. Clumsy person
27. ___ fide
28. Like a 911 call: Abbr.
29. Icicle-like cave deposit
30. Belief
34. Person who's behaviour is such that it should be imitated (4.5)
36. Certain league: Abbr.
37. Tax
39. Rot
41. Four score and ten
44. Camera type, briefly
46. Some batteries
49. "Yoo-hoo!"
51. Some speech sounds
52. Something educed
53. Great
54. Glacial ice formation
58. French novelist Pierre
60. Disney's "___ and the Detectives"
61. Donate
62. Beats by tennis service
64. Duke's grp.
65. "___ won't!"

Puzzle 18

ACROSS

1. Loose fiber used for caulking
6. Civil War general
11. Babe
14. Large wading bird
15. Append
16. Mama bear, in Madrid
17. A fib
19. "Oysters ___ season"
20. Hautboy
21. Family name at Indy
22. At sea
23. Little, e.g.
25. Smirks
27. Thick soup of crabmeat
31. Sundae topper, perhaps
32. "Not ___ bet!"
33. Thick slices
35. Savoury
38. Person in authority
40. Hatred
42. Former Governor General, Sir John -
43. Darkness
45. "Love Story" author
47. Fish eggs
48. Gambol
50. Stately Spanish dance
52. Non-professional
55. Italian capital
56. Vow
57. Johnny ___, "Key Largo" gangster
59. Knots
63. 17th letter of the Greek alphabet
64. Asian country
66. Road surfacing
67. Wash
68. Hips
69. ___ Khan
70. ___ Haute, Ind.
71. Beginning

DOWN

1. Prefix, eight
2. Semite
3. Corn syrup brand
4. Imaginary
5. "Give ___ break!"
6. Arteries
7. Finishes
8. South American mountains
9. Actress Dolores
10. Computer file suffix
11. Shoot-'em-up
12. Willow
13. Grandmothers
18. Art of dueling
22. More or less vertical
24. Dance step
26. Missus
27. D.C. group
28. Indigo
29. Place where experiments take place
30. Awards since 1956
34. Chief source of sugar
36. Press clothes
37. 1856 Stowe novel
39. Truth (Archaic)
41. Leave stranded
44. Abbr. on a French envelope
46. Thrash
49. Ornamental border
51. "Soap" spinoff
52. Major artery
53. Taj ___
54. Jolly - , Pirate's flag
58. Scorch
60. "Miss ___ Regrets"
61. Inhabitant of Denmark
62. Current month
64. Play division
65. 1969 Peace Prize grp.

ACROSS
1. Weary
6. Cape
11. "Think" sloganeer
14. Certain Arab
15. Garlic-flavored mayonnaise
16. "Love Story" composer Francis
17. Association
19. Hallucinogenic drug
20. Like some profs.
21. Theater awards
22. Belonging to us
23. Too
25. Item for scraping shoes at entrance
27. Terminus
31. "Me neither"
32. Architect I. M. ____
33. Light meal
35. Last
38. 3 Sit for portrait
40. Beer mug
42. Title
43. Ignores
45. ____ Island National Monument
47. As yet unscheduled: Abbr.
48. Musical symbol

50. Style of speech
52. Noisy party
55. Daughter of Zeus
56. Perfume name
57. Graf rival
59. Delete (Printing)
63. "Exodus" character
64. Amused
66. Fled
67. Bribe
68. A continuation (3-2)
69. Line part: Abbr.
70. Monetary unit of Poland
71. Appliance maker

DOWN
1. Drink to excess
2. Officiating priest of a mosque
3. Admirable
4. Ensnare
5. Racket
6. Salt of carbonic acid
7. Actress Virna
8. ____ and aahed
9. Novelist Lurie
10. Two-up bat
11. Persons who claim superior enlightenment
12. Iraqi port
13. Amid
18. Red dyes
22. Sen. Hatch

24. "____ Olvidados" (1950 Luis Buñuel film)
26. Money (Slang)
27. "The Mod Squad" co-star, 1999
28. Lighting gas
29. Separating
30. Immune response orchestrator
34. Unit of frequency
36. Early pulpit
37. Thin
39. Black wood
41. Most pleasant
44. Avg.
46. Underwater craft
49. Disney head
51. Monotony
52. Old wound marks
53. Greek goddesses of the seasons
54. Affect
58. Grasslands
60. Sicilian resort
61. Boxer Spinks
62. Dame - Everage, Humphries' character
64. Ovum
65. ____-A (drug used to treat chickenpox)

Puzzle 20

ACROSS
1. Got up
6. African antelope
10. Dunce
14. Mathematician Kurt
15. Not closed
16. Comic strip "___ & Janis"
17. Who "ever loved you more than I," in song
18. Bags
19. The maple
20. The act of immigrating
23. Vandal
24. "Turandot" slave girl
25. Ancient galley
27. Boundary umpire (Football)
32. Hydrocarbon suffixes
33. Conductor ___-Pekka Salonen
34. Get ready to drive
36. "Cómo ___?"
39. "Six Feet Under" son
41. Knob-like
43. ___ II (razor brand)
44. Giraffe-like animal
46. Brings home
48. Altar in the sky
49. Nervous twitches
51. Remembered
53. Near
56. Yoko -
57. Celtic sea god
58. Repeat
64. ___ the Red
66. Hire
67. Light wood
68. Disgusting
69. "___ chance!"
70. "Enigma Variations" composer
71. Hour
72. "The Dukes of Hazzard" spinoff
73. Find out

DOWN
1. Lambs: Lat.
2. Space
3. Baseball's Blue Moon
4. Infirm through old age
5. Author or deliverer of a funeral oration
6. Hawaii's ___ Coast
7. ___ the crack of dawn
8. - and credit
9. Not painful
10. Bleat
11. Resembling an orchestra
12. Fuming sulphuric acid
13. Carried
21. Cud
22. Number of Muses
26. Pause
27. Carson's successor
28. Author Dinesen
29. Swimming pool
30. Great age
31. Less clothed
35. Meat paste
37. River in central Switzerland
38. Great quantity
40. Certain Prot.
42. Maj.'s superior
45. "Happy Birthday" writer
47. Florida island
50. "Tristram Shandy" author
52. Locality
53. Fissure
54. "Vive ___!"
55. Greek theatre
59. To
60. Fund-raising grps.
61. Aquatic plant
62. Former Russian ruler
63. Merit
65. Diminutive suffix

40

Puzzle 21

ACROSS
1. Eating desk
6. Metal dross
10. Probability
14. Subtle emanations
15. Fleet rodent
16. Arduous journey
17. Clarification lead-in
18. Cause of scratching
19. Banks on the runway
20. Crust of the earth
23. Floor rug
24. Big picture?: Abbr.
25. Read to a stenographer
27. What M. can stand for
32. Apparently successful project
33. Revised form of Esperanto
34. Concerned with a specific subject
36. Leave undisturbed (3.2)
39. Women, slangily
41. "Calvin and Hobbes" girl
43. Actress Sorvino
44. Does not succeed
46. Harts' mates
48. Guy Fawkes Day mo.
49. Soft lambskin leather
51. Make equal
53. Asexual

reproductive cell
56. Economic stat.
57. Gun (Slang)
58. Cluster together
64. Rent-a-car company
66. Ark builder
67. Gulf of Aqaba port
68. Literally, "numbered"
69. "Crimes and Misdemeanors" actor
70. Severe
71. Pond dweller
72. Aspiring atty.'s exam
73. Journalist Alexander

DOWN
1. Appendage
2. Autobahn auto
3. Cy Young winner Saberhagen
4. Whips
5. It regained independence in 1991
6. Ocean craft
7. Slat
8. Bowed
9. Baseball's all-time leader in grand slams
10. His "4" was retired
11. Bond order
12. Rid of vermin
13. Perform on ice
21. Toboggans

22. Biol. branch
26. Abound
27. Vex
28. Ancient theaters
29. Putting forward a person's name for election
30. "Don't think so"
31. First name in talk shows
35. Roulette bet
37. Josip ___ (Marshal Tito's original name)
38. Roof overhang
40. Close hard
42. Draw forth
45. Particular, for short
47. Withered
50. Discordant
52. Female demon in Semitic myth
53. Brightly coloured lizard
54. Auctioneer's hammer
55. Organic compounds
59. Thompson of "Family"
60. This thing
61. Epithet of Athena
62. Mountain lake
63. Sicilian volcano
65. Large body of water

Puzzle 22

ACROSS

1. Parasitic insects
6. Lowest high tide
10. Film rating org.
14. Rimes of country music
15. Prefix, eight
16. Circular plate
17. Unbind
18. Olio
19. Old injury mark
20. Short-legged hound
23. Comedian Margaret
24. Suffix with mock
25. Relate
27. Adorned, in a way
32. British nobleman
33. Coll. in Troy, N.Y.
34. Edited out
36. Riviera, e.g.
39. Is not
41. Wandered
43. Australian super-model
44. "Taras Bulba" author
46. Canon competitor
48. Haul
49. On top of
51. Bequests
53. Eating

disturbance
56. Actress Scala
57. Biochemistry abbr.
58. Preventing fever
64. Frigid finish
66. "Das Lied von der ___"
67. 1970 World's Fair site
68. Grasp
69. Uproar
70. Nobleman
71. Greek war goddess
72. "Do the Right Thing" pizzeria
73. "The Faerie Queene" character

DOWN

1. Bungle
2. Olin of "Chocolat"
3. Food
4. Liqueur flavorers
5. Derided
6. Food
7. Plasm prefix
8. Depleted
9. Oklahoma Indian
10. "ER" roles
11. Relish
12. Japanese beer brand
13. Canton neighbor

21. First president to marry while in office
22. Dull
26. Authentic
27. H.S. class
28. Lhasa ___
29. Remarkably
30. Carolina college
31. Demon
35. Apollo astronaut Slayton
37. A hint
38. Beer barrels
40. Pith helmet
42. Pet term for dog
45. ___ Linda, Calif.
47. Capital of Kenya
50. NFL team, for short
52. Roman general
53. Astronomer Tycho
54. Federation
55. Courtyards
59. Object of worship
60. Guinea pigs, maybe
61. Noxious weed
62. Religious image: Var.
63. Scene of first miracle
65. Tokyo, formerly

44

ACROSS

1. Gaels
6. Pouches
10. Mex. miss
14. Sacred: Prefix
15. Funeral notice
16. Neither masc. nor fem.
17. Spinning
18. Cartel city
19. Land measure
20. Ending
23. Baseball card stat.
24. Wood sorrel
25. Mutually accept
27. Dreadful
32. Big name in games
33. Open
34. Puccini opera
36. Like some communities
39. Wallace of Reader's Digest
41. Red variety of spinel
43. Dreadful
44. The Sorbonne, e.g.
46. Lake in the Sierra Nevada
48. Poem
49. Quote
51. Russian empresses
53. Clattering noise
56. Neighbor of Mo.
57. Consume
58. Capable of being addressed
64. Opera solo
66. Protection
67. Fencing equipment
68. Bus. bigwigs
69. Undermines
70. Rent out again
71. Female birds
72. Forest growth
73. Ante

DOWN

1. Natter
2. Ireland
3. Ogle
4. Slight trembling
5. Tout
6. Caribbean dance music
7. Blind as ___
8. Eyelashes
9. Smarts
10. Simple fastener
11. A pastime
12. Prefix, turbine
13. Saved on supper, perhaps
21. Wealthy person
22. Diver Louganis
26. Minor oath
27. Lacquered metalware
28. Heroic
29. Act of moving to a new place
30. Future atty.'s exam
31. Applause
35. Exclamations of surprise
37. "Das Rheingold" goddess
38. Bad marks
40. Got down from mount
42. Saturates
45. Bluesy James
47. Rubbers
50. Oldest
52. All worked up
53. Seashore
54. ___ show
55. Mystery writer's award
59. Mature
60. Sum, ___, fui
61. Actor Lugosi
62. Welsh emblem
63. Punta del ___, Uruguay
65. Donkey

47

Puzzle 24

ACROSS

1. Exposed
6. False god
10. Capital of Western Samoa
14. Purgative injection
15. Boss on a shield
16. 3 Weapons
17. Strand, in a way
18. Explorer John and others
19. Frosh, next year
20. Hypermetropic (4-7)
23. ___ Dee River
24. Confederate soldier, for short
25. Meat cut
27. Coffeecake topping
32. Row
33. "... ___ quit!"
34. "Walk Away ___" (1966 hit)
36. Flower part
39. Revenuers
41. Montana, e.g., once
43. Prefix, Chinese
44. Of an axis
46. Levees
48. "Put ___ Happy Face"
49. 1989 Literature Nobelist
51. Allocated
53. Becomes noisier
56. Exclamation of surprise
57. Immigrant's class: Abbr.
58. Trivial
64. Small particle
66. When repeated, a fish
67. Gravel ridge
68. Prefix with -algia
69. ___ Bator, Mongolia
70. Stalks
71. Proboscis
72. Sensible
73. "Ah, Wilderness!" mother

DOWN

1. Trompe l'___
2. Remarkable
3. Adolescent
4. An American in Paris, maybe
5. Male ballet dancer
6. Quiet town
7. Asian nurse
8. Wrongfully assists
9. Come unglued
10. Walkman batteries
11. Ratio
12. L'Enfant Plaza designer
13. Wan
21. Norwegian dramatist
22. Drop moisture
26. Dregs
27. Divan
28. "Jurassic Park" menace
29. Absurd
30. "Idylls of the King" lady
31. Actress Lotte
35. Fun house sounds
37. Author Rice
38. A burden
40. Sledge
42. Iterate
45. Gr. 1-6
47. Thai
50. Hostility
52. Spectres
53. Singer Rimes
54. Prefix, bone
55. La ___
59. Persian lord
60. "___ kleine Nachtmusik"
61. Hawaiian strings
62. Prefix, part
63. Scottish Gaelic
65. G.I. chow in Desert Storm

Puzzle 25

ACROSS

1. Tablets
6. Capital of Togo
10. Bargain event
14. Negatively charged ion
15. King Harald's father
16. Movie-rating org.
17. Mediterranean island
18. Recent: Prefix
19. Datebook abbr.
20. On - , In a state of anxiety
23. Estuary
24. "... ___ quit!"
25. Closest
27. Rubs
32. Anthropologist Fossey
33. Malt beverage
34. Seasoning herb
36. Stringed instruments
39. Sharp ringing sound
41. Lachrymal drops
43. Italian currency
44. Sober
46. Removed moisture
48. Geom. figure
49. "Gone With the Wind" plantation
51. Covering
53. "Call!"
56. Bygone money
57. Always, in verse
58. Dunces
64. "National Velvet" author Bagnold
66. Future J.D.'s hurdle
67. Bar, legally
68. March Madness org.
69. Wallaroo
70. Escarpment
71. Vend
72. Adolescent
73. Measured

DOWN

1. Agreement
2. About, on a memo
3. Charge over property
4. Numbers games
5. Pooh-pooh
6. Scottish lake
7. Blue Bonnet, e.g.
8. Massenet opera
9. Called forth
10. Little, in Leith
11. Trade student
12. ___ lazuli
13. Patronize, as a restaurant
21. Correct
22. Travel on water
26. Actor Julia
27. Charts
28. Got down from mount
29. Consisting of senators
30. Looked over
31. Clever
35. A Great Lake
37. Ireland
38. Muralist José María ___
40. Composer ___ Carlo Menotti
42. Rocker Bob
45. 1856 Stowe novel
47. Duke's wife
50. Talisman
52. Breakfast mixture of grains, fruit, and nuts
53. Hammer parts
54. Therefore
55. Follow
59. Challenge
60. English public school
61. Complete
62. Drugs
63. Raced
65. Indian dish

Puzzle 26

ACROSS
1. Water wheel
6. Bygone auto
10. Bile
14. Funeral notices
15. A Great Lake
16. Dagger
17. Perch
18. Clump of trees
19. Amenhotep IV's god
20. Definite
23. Also
24. Ballot abbr.
25. Impartial
27. Silver coin equal to five cents
32. Actor Stoltz
33. Single unit
34. Wear away
36. Available
39. "Miracle" team of 1969
41. Woman with ___
43. Hokkaido native
44. 10th-century Holy Roman emperor
46. Ant
48. Automobile
49. Hearing organs
51. Part
53. Having cirri
56. "Do Ya" rock grp.
57. Fire remains
58. Argumentative
64. South African
66. American Indian
67. F.D.R.'s Interior Secretary
68. Astronaut Shepard
69. To yield
70. "Honest"
71. Youths
72. Chances
73. Approaches

DOWN
1. L'Étoile du ___, Minnesota's motto
2. Musical instrument
3. Public disturbance
4. Emphatic form of it
5. Straddling
6. Moore of "G.I. Jane"
7. "East of Eden" brother
8. Giant
9. Divan
10. Fed. construction overseer
11. Most southerly continent
12. Hotelier Helmsley
13. U.S. Open champ, 1985-87
21. African musical instrument
22. Wallaroo
26. Louise of "Gilligan's Island"
27. - sapiens, Man
28. Without ___ (dangerously)
29. Printed heading on stationery
30. Sulk
31. Dutch exports
35. Salinger girl
37. Biol. subject
38. Chaste
40. Fly high
42. Wigwam
45. Republic in SW Asia
47. Capital of Estonia
50. Coarse plaster
52. Pistol, slangily
53. Intrigue
54. Capri, e.g.
55. Having ears
59. Spawning area of salmon
60. Roger of "Cheers"
61. Tex. neighbor
62. Israel's Golda
63. Go-aheads
65. "ER" extras

Puzzle 27

ACROSS
1. Brace
6. Terror
10. Collections
14. Artillery sighter
15. Tennis star, - Natase
16. Fam. tree member
17. Bambino watcher
18. Guesses: Abbr.
19. Prefix, ten
20. Beardless
23. Hazy
24. "Give ___ rest!"
25. Cleft lip
27. Black bird
32. Club-like weapon
33. Babe
34. Castilian hero
36. Succeed
39. Food
41. 3 Banked money
43. Wallace of Reader's Digest
44. "Let's Make ___"
46. Race of Norse gods
48. Japanese word of respect
49. Prompts
51. Bullet that rebounds from struck surface
53. Clergyman
56. Antipollution org.
57. Boy
58. Plan beforehand
64. Fruity coolers
66. Periods of history
67. An anaesthetic
68. One of Columbus's ships
69. River deposit
70. Jargon
71. Packs
72. Pip
73. Trials

DOWN
1. Machine parts
2. Actor Neeson
3. Ammunition (Colloq)
4. Autobiography
5. Chatter
6. Fee
7. "Born Free" lioness
8. 8th letter
9. Do some tailoring
10. Sum
11. The gar
12. Computer acronym
13. Rogue
21. Greets
22. Haul
26. Biol. branch
27. 2000 World Series locale
28. Amphibian
29. Prior
30. Org. with eligibility rules
31. Donor
35. He loved Lucy
37. Wings: Lat.
38. Rave
40. First king of Israel
42. Cubed
45. Jump
47. Most fibrous
50. Emphasis
52. Cows
53. Board placed on trestles
54. Pie cuts, essentially
55. Strange and mysterious
59. Man
60. Cornerstone abbr.
61. Cries of surprise
62. Camp shelter
63. Work units
65. Airline to Stockholm

Puzzle 28

ACROSS

1. Rush-like plant
6. Prefix, ten
10. Bric-a-___
14. "He's ___ nowhere man" (Beatles lyric)
15. Native Nigerians
16. Network
17. "Kate & ___"
18. A long, long time
19. Assuming that's true
20. Financial analyst
23. Cyclades island
24. Aliens, for short
25. Embellish
27. Pertaining to geodesy
32. Prefix, distant
33. Part of a circle
34. Made fancy
36. Draw a bead on
39. Flaky mineral
41. Actor Lew
43. Ward of "Once and Again"
44. Glide along smoothly
46. Slants
48. Naught
49. Situate
51. Theatrical
53. Leaf appendage
56. "Krazy ___"
57. ___ system
58. Aimlessness

64. Left
66. ___ Mujeres, Mexico
67. Rather, informally
68. Collections
69. Düsseldorf denial
70. Grain fungus
71. Vend
72. Couturier Cassini
73. Brings up

DOWN

1. Auto import
2. "House of Frankenstein" director ___ C. Kenton
3. Boxing's Oscar ___ Hoya
4. Profited by
5. Chose
6. "Mon ___!"
7. Black
8. Fable
9. Agree
10. Ascap alternative
11. An improvement
12. Org.
13. Selected
21. Old Roman port
22. Ostrichlike bird
26. "Aladdin" prince and namesakes

27. Legs, slangily
28. Estrada of "CHiPs"
29. Infrequent
30. Romantic interlude
31. Remedied
35. Pome
37. Others, in Latin
38. Fine powder
40. Eagerly expectant
42. Reptile
45. Sewing case
47. Dollar
50. Warming of south Pacific causing Australian drought (2.4)
52. Dress
53. Heroic stories
54. Choice steak (1-4)
55. 50's Ford flop
59. Tennis star, - Natase
60. Phoned
61. "Young Frankenstein" woman
62. Scent
63. Turner and others
65. Immigrant's course: Abbr.

Puzzle 29

ACROSS
1. Indian guitar-like instrument
6. "The Last of the Mohicans" girl
10. Kraft Nabisco Championship org.
14. Province of central Spain
15. "Voice of Israel" author
16. "High Hopes" lyricist
17. Massenet opera
18. American grey wolf
19. Damn
20. Captivating
23. "Aladdin" prince
24. Atmosphere
25. Energetic
27. Serial instalments
32. ___ Hari
33. My, French (Plural)
34. "I cannot ___ lie"
36. Early weather satellite
39. Form of ether
41. Christmas songs
43. Mound
44. Sprints
46. Author Zora ___ Hurston
48. Metal rod
49. Principal
51. Cheap copy
53. Loitered
56. Fem. pronoun
57. Daughter of Cadmus
58. Tenant under a lease
64. Years abroad
66. Dr.'s orders
67. Ex of the Donald
68. Genuine
69. Old cloth measures
70. Coming between 8 and 10
71. Wheel shaft
72. Florida's Miami-___ County
73. Growls

DOWN
1. Identical
2. "Terrible" czar
3. Hue
4. Warm welcomes
5. Cut loose
6. Prison room
7. Ancient Greek coin
8. Frenzied
9. Assumed name
10. Digital readout, for short
11. Capital of Suriname
12. Diplomat Boutros Boutros-___
13. Caper
21. Cosmetician Elizabeth
22. Biting insect
26. On one's toes
27. Part of E.M.T.: Abbr.
28. Elizabeth of "La Bamba"
29. Uniform in time
30. North Carolina college
31. Smooth and glossy
35. Broadway's ___ Jay Lerner
37. Count played by Jim Carrey in "Lemony Snicket's A Series of Unfortunate Events"
38. Slave
40. Sly look
42. Splash through mud
45. Put to sea
47. Resounding
50. Thought
52. Absolute scale of temperature
53. Coronet
54. Addition
55. "Our Gang" girl
59. Immature herring
60. They, in Trieste
61. "Two Years Before the Mast" writer
62. ___'acte (intermission)
63. Cheers
65. Island (France)

Puzzle 30

ACROSS
1. Watered garden
6. Epiphanies
10. Photo
13. Proprietor
14. East Indies palm
15. 20th letter of the Hebrew alphabet
16. Purposeful
18. ___ Stanley Gardner
19. Chang's Siamese twin
20. Adriatic port
21. 1994 Peace Nobelist
23. "Dear" advice-giver
24. Formula of belief
25. Contacts quickly, perhaps
28. Tarried
31. Wilkes-___, Pa.
32. Washed
33. Critic ___ Louise Huxtable
34. Parting words
35. Took by force
36. Busy
37. Long period of time
38. Packs down
39. White poplar tree
40. Euros replaced them
42. Went in the direction of

43. Restrains
44. Atmosphere
45. Unsaturated alcohol
47. Boatswain
48. Possessed
51. Sainted pope called "the Great"
52. Unfitness
55. Quito's country: Abbr.
56. Goddess of victory
57. Sponsorship
58. Some batters, for short
59. Showy ornament
60. Mother-in-law of Ruth

DOWN
1. Abode
2. Submachine gun
3. Obstacle
4. Even (poet.)
5. Slobber
6. Irate
7. High fidelity
8. Kwik-E-Mart clerk on "The Simpsons"
9. Receiving a salary
10. Pierced with holes
11. ___ Mujeres, Mexico
12. Jazz trumpeter Baker

15. Aptly named English novelist
17. Captures
22. Abbr. after many a general's name
23. Affectation
24. Bays
25. Waned
26. City leader
27. Sandy
28. Arctic dwellers
29. Ancient Roman magistrate
30. Outmoded
32. Tibetan monks
35. Wandering
36. In ___ way
38. "Comin' ___ the Rye"
39. Eternal
41. Papal court
42. Party holder
44. Sulked
45. Toboggan
46. Technical college (Colloq)
47. Capital of Azerbaijan
48. "Les Miserables" author
49. Take ___ view of
50. Lucie's brother
53. Actress Vardalos of "My Big Fat Greek Wedding"
54. Light meal

60

Puzzle 30

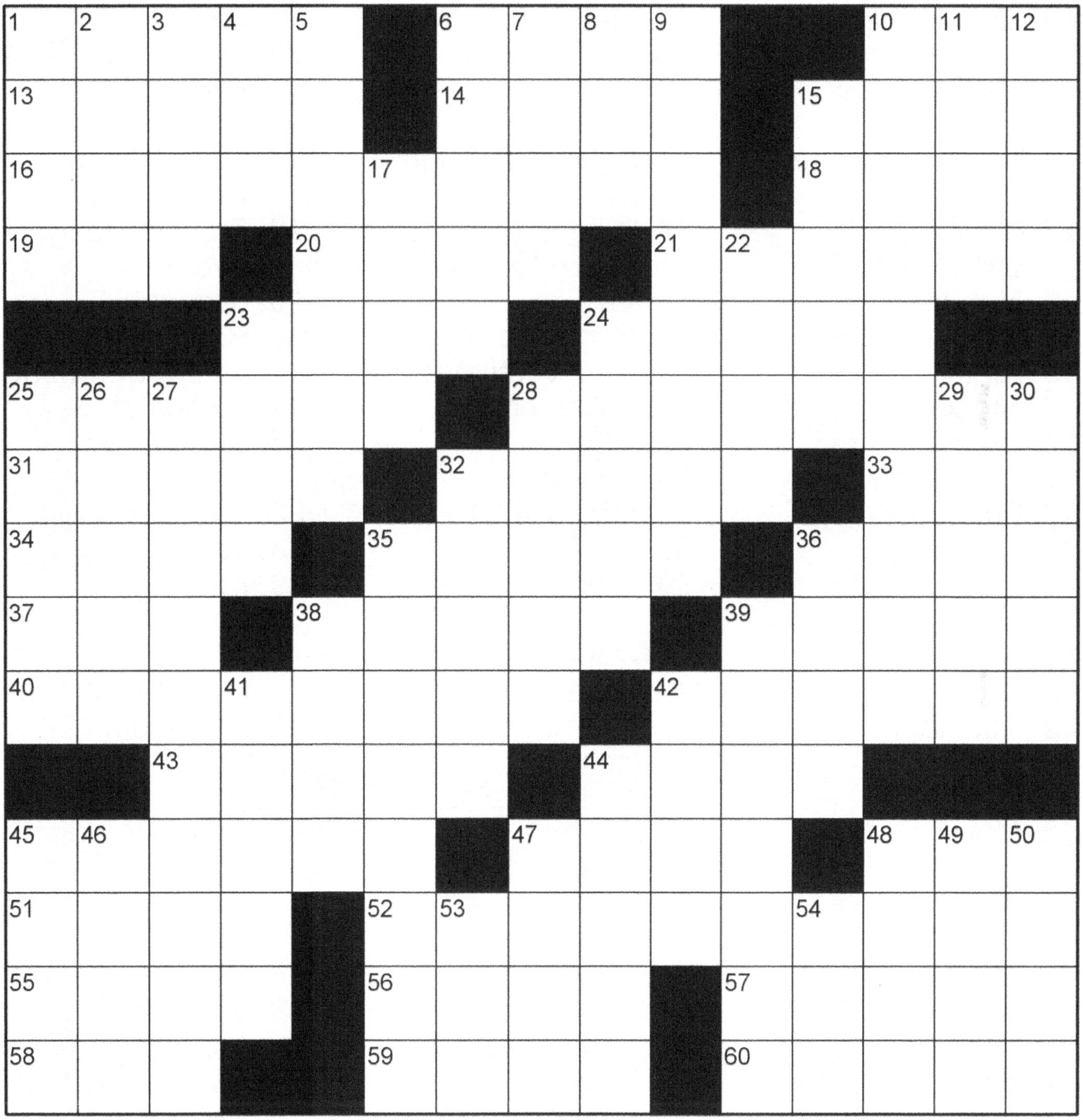
1
2
3
4
5
6
7
8
9
10
11
12
13
14
15
16
17
18
19
20
21
22
23
24
25
26
27
28
29
30
31
32
33
34
35
36
37
38
39
40
41
42
43
44
45
46
47
48
49
50
51
52
53
54
55
56
57
58
59
60

Puzzle 31

ACROSS
1. Gossipy Hopper
6. Bleats
10. Even if, briefly
13. - Welles, actor, producer, and director
14. Stove or washer: Abbr.
15. "Moby Dick" captain
16. Not rifled
18. Recent: Prefix
19. Airline to Stockholm
20. Burden
21. Come to light
23. Funhouse cries
24. ___ citato
25. Like some bands
28. Nonchalant (4-4)
31. Smart - , show-offs
32. Fountain orders
33. Ingot
34. Whip
35. More underhanded
36. He sang "I've Got You Under My Skin" with Frank Sinatra on "Duets"
37. Six-pointers, for short
38. Oak nut
39. European brown bear
40. An amorous glance
42. Missouri feeder
43. Marine mammals
44. Performance by two
45. Cursed
47. Acquire through merit
48. "Silent" prez
51. Sacred image: Var.
52. Component part
55. Well ventilated
56. Indian bread
57. Waned
58. Direction opposite SSW
59. Sets
60. Disorderly flights

DOWN
1. "Bonanza" brother
2. "Aunt" with a "Cope Book"
3. Brit. decorations
4. Scooby-___ (cartoon dog)
5. Deer's horns
6. Rum cakes
7. Snake, for one
8. 30-day mo.
9. More drowsy
10. Near that place
11. Drape
12. Hautboy
15. Biting
17. Jazz (up)
22. Drugs, briefly
23. Every
24. Like some old buckets
25. Finnish architect Alvar ___
26. Knife
27. Mies van der Rohe's motto
28. France's longest river
29. "Enough!"
30. Basic monetary unit of Denmark
32. Lumps of clay
35. Burning with water
36. Impudent child
38. Wings: Lat.
39. Kitchen appliance
41. 1974 title role for Dustin Hoffman
42. Free from contamination
44. Mends socks
45. Anthropologist Fossey
46. Related by blood
47. Alike: Fr.
48. Philippine island
49. Without ___ (daringly)
50. Former Fords
53. Not
54. Nigerian tribesman

Puzzle 32

ACROSS

1. Detective Pinkerton
6. Blind as ___
10. "Yo te ___"
13. Magnifying glass used by jewelers
14. Boxer Oscar ___ Hoya
15. Among
16. Applies oil or grease
18. Clublike weapon
19. Cooler
20. Spanish appetizer
21. Having stabiliser fin
23. Closed
24. Blowing away
25. Humperdinck heroine
28. Five Nations tribe
31. Enthusiastic
32. Key personnel
33. ___ school
34. Confess
35. Fabric hand-dyeing technique
36. Tabula ___
37. ___ room
38. Eastern wrap
39. One of the Reagans
40. Railway ties
42. Go at full speed
43. Indigent
44. Hill of "The West Wing"
45. Potsdam Conference attendee
47. Yours and mine
48. "Sprechen ___ Deutsch?"
51. Naked
52. Benevolence
55. Footnote abbr.
56. 90° from norte
57. Wallaroos
58. Computer key: Abbr.
59. Frat letters
60. "Cheers" role

DOWN

1. "It was ___ mistake!"
2. Noisy
3. Lubricate
4. 30-day mo.
5. Not any of two
6. Change to suit
7. Greek letter
8. Beer
9. Piecework
10. Merge
11. Small rodents
12. Had too much, briefly
15. Alter
17. Hood-like membrane
22. Article in Der Spiegel
23. Olio
24. Actress MacDowell
25. Toothed wheels
26. Entangle
27. Self-centred
28. "Bellefleur" author
29. "Beau ___"
30. Firefighter Red
32. Tote
35. Guidebook for travelers
36. Uncommon
38. Graf ___
39. Paralysed
41. Caught congers
42. Ringlet
44. Dandies
45. "___ Baby" (song from "Hair")
46. Labels
47. Upon
48. "Buona ___" (Italian greeting)
49. "The heat ___!"
50. They, in Trieste
53. Book end?
54. Rapa ___ (Easter Island)

Puzzle 33

ACROSS
1. Cooked in oil
6. Cartoonist Addams
10. Father
13. Aegean region
14. Matured
15. Staple Oriental grain
16. Restored to office
18. Ballpark figs.
19. Superlative suffix
20. Crones
21. Asexual
23. Island rings
24. Musical study piece
25. San ___, Calif.
28. Employee of a dairy
31. Bring into line
32. Horn-shaped bone
33. Buddy
34. The villain in Othello
35. Tine
36. Ursa
37. "Rugrats" dad
38. Cries for attention
39. Pavement edges
40. Weirdness
42. Existing
43. Opera solos
44. "The Plague" city
45. Giants
47. Antarctica's Prince ___ Coast
48. Black bird
51. Ireland
52. Direct
55. Sitar master Shankar
56. Something not to be done (2-2)
57. Ballroom dance
58. British verb ending
59. Specific thing indicated
60. "Siddhartha" author

DOWN
1. Flame
2. Some deer
3. Arctic native
4. "Ich bin ___ Berliner"
5. Taro
6. Rocky heights
7. Strikes
8. Primate
9. Tranquillising
10. Deprives of limbs
11. Broadway opening
12. Fam. tree member
15. Prepared
17. Hindmost part of an animal
22. Hindu teacher
23. Titicaca, por ejemplo
24. Works for
25. Lift
26. Winged
27. Metaphorical
28. Ill-fates
29. Semites
30. Scandinavian
32. Salad herb
35. Game bird
36. "Has - ". Person who once was
38. Have ___ (be connected)
39. Dishonest
41. Khomeini, for one
42. Republic in SW Asia
44. Hodgepodges
45. Austin of "Knots Landing"
46. Nest eggs, briefly
47. Former home to the Hawks, with "the"
48. 24-hr. conveniences
49. Beaks
50. "Dies ___"
53. Scale note
54. Freelancer's enc.

Puzzle 34

ACROSS

1. Pertaining to the ileum
6. Sgts., e.g.
10. Fu-___ (legendary Chinese sage)
13. Roman general
14. "East of Eden" director Kazan
15. Great age
16. Invention
18. Foolish
19. First word of Dante's "Inferno"
20. Novice
21. Skillful
23. Proper name in Masses
24. Of punishment
25. Classify
28. Punish
31. Inventor Howe
32. Graduated glass tube
33. Rummy game
34. ___ Féin
35. Loathed
36. "Curses!"
37. Prefix with meter
38. Female relatives
39. Deadly
40. Large-billed birds
42. Ancient Iran

43. Humdingers
44. Pardner's mount
45. Oriental temple
47. Coal dust
48. New Deal inits.
51. "Q ___ queen"
52. Managed
55. Be defeated
56. Cure
57. Kind of board
58. Often
59. Nervous
60. East Indies palms

DOWN

1. Library ID
2. Tempt
3. Carrier whose name means "skyward"
4. "Mârouf" baritone
5. Fast horse gaits
6. First prime minister of India
7. History Muse
8. Petroleum
9. Made morose
10. Motor vehicle lights
11. Couch
12. Like JFK
15. "You've got ___!"
17. Prehistoric sepulchral tomb
22. Gray matter?: Abbr.

23. ___ of Arc
24. Fathers
25. Greek writer of fables
26. Slip
27. Specialist in Sinology
28. Golf strokes
29. Mountain where Moses received the law
30. "Waterworld" girl
32. Notice of an intended marriage
35. Mexican sandal
36. Rowing implements
38. Beaten by tennis service
39. Decorate
41. Combined
42. Indigent
44. Torridly
45. ___ Alto, Calif.
46. Beginning
47. Catch
48. Turn over
49. ___ vu
50. Nutritional info
53. Brit. lexicon
54. George Sand's "Elle et ___"

Puzzle 35

ACROSS
1. Camera setting
6. Death rattle
10. Small batteries
13. Stews
14. Egyptian solar deity
15. M.'s counterpart
16. Preceding marriage
18. Olive genus
19. Kazakhstan, once: Abbr.
20. Waterfall
21. Silvery white
23. Tiny, informally
24. German, war
25. Meal course
28. Divide into pages
31. "The Merry Widow" composer
32. "___ Johnny!"
33. Rx instruction
34. Lake
35. Relaxed
36. Liquid secreted by the liver
37. Fuss
38. Power line tower
39. Introduction
40. Beautiful young maidens
42. Bantu language
43. Lures
44. River crossing
45. Persons in general

47. Chill
48. Explorer Johnson
51. Tabula ___
52. Voting district
55. Wicked
56. Spanish appetizer
57. Imply
58. "Der Ring ___ Nibelungen"
59. Foot part
60. Spiteful

DOWN
1. Dandies
2. Some cameras: Abbr.
3. Stratum
4. South Africa's ___ Paul Kruger
5. Psalmbook
6. Descriptive of wet weather
7. Abbr. on an envelope
8. Meadow
9. Expanded
10. Assertion made without proof
11. Architect William Van ___
12. Chair
15. ___ David
17. Ascend
22. "How the Other Half Lives" author
23. Dies ___

24. "From Here to Eternity" wife
25. Jazz trumpeter Ziggy
26. Destitute
27. Blood clots in the veins
28. Mexican monetary units
29. Covered with ceramic pieces
30. Dropsy
32. Stops
35. Canine teeth
36. A nail
38. "Murphy Brown" bar owner
39. Steal
41. Of a pontiff
42. Underground part of a plant
44. Of focus
45. Sentence part: Abbr.
46. Overhanging lower edge of a roof
47. French chef's mushroom
48. Blockheads
49. Printer's mark, keep
50. Ethereal
53. New Guinea seaport
54. Biology class abbr.

Puzzle 36

ACROSS
1. Snoops
6. Hindu titles
10. Pen point
13. Containing iodine
14. Blackjack
15. One of Columbus's ships
16. It may be pulled
18. Monster
19. Annoying insect
20. ___ Valley, Calif.
21. Book before Job
23. ___ buco
24. Writer of lyric poetry
25. Container in which infusions are made
28. Lightest element
31. Bring on oneself
32. Wheel hubs
33. Bullfight call
34. Red planet
35. Struck out
36. Bushman's pack
37. Ear: Prefix
38. Hero of 1898
39. African tribe
40. Paints again
42. Pretenses
43. Composted soil
44. Successful runners, for short
45. Scratched
47. Spool
48. ___ Victor
51. Sunscreen ingredient
52. Specter
55. Husk
56. Highland toppers
57. 1977 George Burns film
58. Narc's org.
59. Gaelic
60. African antelope

DOWN
1. "La Vie en Rose" singer
2. Trundle
3. Lazily
4. A, overseas
5. Cut with scissors
6. Bonehead
7. Indian bread
8. Expert finish
9. Finely chopped
10. Garments worn usually just before going to bed
11. About, on a memo
12. 1930's heavyweight champ Max
15. "Au contraire!"
17. Pith
22. Knights' titles
23. Musical work
24. Words of dismay
25. Malay island
26. Related on one's mother's side
27. Fear of heights
28. Pulls
29. Overjoy
30. Hot wine drink
32. Efts
35. Make bare
36. "Je ne ___ quoi"
38. American coin
39. Gold or silver ingots
41. Pertaining to the ear
42. Apparently successful project
44. Porridge ingredient
45. W.W. I plane
46. Attention
47. Tach readings
48. Baltic capital
49. Moderately cold
50. "Shave ___ haircut"
53. Normal
54. Your

72

Puzzle 37

ACROSS
1. Climbing vine
6. Sale caveat
10. 11-member grp.
13. Embed
14. "Born Free" lioness
15. Expressed surprise
16. Treatise
18. Uncover
19. "Bambi" character
20. Singer k. d. ___
21. Danish city
23. Mandlikova of tennis
24. Golfer Sam
25. Melodic passage
28. Stealers of game
31. Freshwater food fish
32. Artist Matisse
33. Hawaii's Mauna ___
34. Chunk
35. Altar stone
36. Spear point
37. Spanish bear
38. Backside
39. Unripe
40. Coarse wheat meal
42. Cricket sounds

43. Satire
44. Top
45. Dug-outs
47. Future doc's exam
48. Twice
51. Arab League member
52. Most parched
55. Affect
56. Agatha contemporary
57. Leered
58. Affirmative vote
59. Merge
60. Feet parts

DOWN
1. Adult nits
2. ___ a good thing
3. "Summer and Smoke" heroine
4. Vietnam
5. Eyelid hair
6. Insurance giant
7. Metal dross
8. Desert land: Abbr.
9. Farewell
10. Decorative light fixture
11. Philly team
12. Chick follower
15. Belief involving sorcery
17. Prefix meaning "one-billionth"

22. Metric prefix
23. Joint in the hind leg of a horse
24. Robust
25. A Musketeer
26. Recycle
27. Nameless
28. Contour feather
29. Weatherman Al
30. Composer Camille Saint-___
32. Funnyman Youngman
35. Trunk
36. Grand ___
38. Floating ice
39. Slum areas
41. Home of the Black Bears
42. Auditors
44. Landed
45. Musical ending
46. Island in the Taiwan Strait
47. Grain factory
48. Gong
49. "Aha"
50. Benchmarks: Abbr.
53. Charlemagne's domain: Abbr.
54. "Here ___ Again" (1987 #1 hit)

Puzzle 38

ACROSS
1. Took by force
6. Obstacle
10. Etcetera
13. Egg-shaped
14. ___ nut
15. Abbr. at the end of a list
16. Inflammation of an ovary
18. Verne's submariner
19. ___ lab
20. "Lovely" Beatles girl
21. Coupled
23. Aaron's 2,297
24. Staff again
25. French underground movement
28. Inferring
31. Enumerate
32. Of the sun
33. ___ el Amarna, Egypt
34. Mardi ___
35. Faithful
36. Prima donna
37. Itinerary abbr.
38. Early form of FAX
39. Belonging to them
40. Native of the planet Earth
42. Gliding dance step
43. Brother of Moses
44. Metal fastener

45. Hit two balls successively in billiards
47. Songwriter Bacharach
48. Driller's org.
51. Actress Diana
52. Illiterate
55. 1968 folk album
56. Author Roald
57. Choose
58. Farewell
59. Guesses: Abbr.
60. Radioactive gaseous element

DOWN
1. Crucifix
2. River in central England
3. Father
4. Addis Ababa's land: Abbr.
5. Leave orbit
6. Short parodies
7. "___ chance"
8. "Prince ___" ("Aladdin" song)
9. Step on it
10. Very long times
11. Domesticate
12. Lump of earth
15. Early computer
17. New York's Jacob ___ Park
22. Russia/Manchuria boundary river
23. Cricket scores

24. Ease
25. John D. MacDonald sleuth Travis ___
26. Major artery
27. Figure having four sides
28. Senior member
29. One of the Leeward Islands
30. Bright glow
32. Gannet
35. Citrus drink
36. Indian pulses
38. "Comin' ___ the Rye"
39. Towards that place
41. Ballroom dance
42. Freshwater fish
44. Negates
45. Crustacean
46. Breezy
47. Monetary unit of Thailand
48. In bed
49. Art ___
50. Business letter abbr.
53. "If I Ruled the World" rapper
54. ___ grecque (cooked in olive oil, lemon juice, wine, and herbs, and served cold)

Puzzle 39

ACROSS
1. Scale
6. Drudge
10. One of the Spice Girls
14. Halogen element
15. Singer
16. Like a 911 call: Abbr.
17. Edges
19. Gospel singer Winans
20. Abilene-to-San Antonio dir.
21. "Get Shorty" novelist Leonard
22. New Jersey's ___ University
23. Western pact
24. Football Hall-of-Famer Jim
26. Places where experiments take place
31. Con men?
32. ___ Sutra
33. "A likely story!"
36. Hood-like membrane
37. Inflect words
39. "A Doll's House" heroine
40. Space invaders, for short
41. Small yeast cake
42. Theory
43. Elucidation
46. Sitting Bull, e.g.
49. Insects
50. Mild oath
51. Irritate
54. Clean Air Act org.
57. Actress Singer of "Footloose"
58. Tyrannical
60. "Mockingbird" singer Foxx
61. Beheaded Boleyn
62. Pelvic bones
63. "Auld Lang ___"
64. Minus
65. Dull

DOWN
1. Little lies
2. Lorelei Lee's creator
3. Together, musically
4. Relation
5. Makes beloved
6. Burrowing rodent
7. Potpourri
8. Aqueduct of Sylvius, e.g.
9. Lollygag
10. Small lizards
11. Arab leader
12. Sum up
13. Greek goddess of peace
18. ___ Loma, Calif.
23. Wool fibre
25. "Isn't ___ bit like you and me?" (Beatles lyric)
26. Openwork fabric
27. Gray's subj.
28. Air conditioner capacity, for short
29. Podded plants
30. ___ Tafari (Haile Selassie)
33. "___ soit qui mal y pense"
34. "Giovanna d'___" (Verdi opera)
35. Chemistry Nobelist Otto
37. Resembling a palace
38. "Aladdin" monkey
39. Crazy (Colloq)
41. Short order, for short
42. Jawless fish
43. Impregnate with iodine
44. Butchers' offerings
45. Lacy neckpiece
46. Delicatessens
47. Severe pain
48. Silkwood of "Silkwood"
52. Sea eagle
53. A dog's age
54. Engrave with acid
55. South American country
56. First man
59. Cracker biscuit

Puzzle 40

ACROSS
1. Dandruff
6. Store
10. Russo of "Get Shorty"
14. Adorable one
15. Scion
16. E.P.A. concern: Abbr.
17. - snowman (Yeti)
19. Attend
20. Like L.B.J.
21. Most secure
22. Hardly haute cuisine
23. "Now!"
24. "Seinfeld" gal
26. Chance happening
31. Grinding tooth
32. Opening run
33. Droop
36. "Don't bet ___!"
37. Outrigger
39. Gape
40. Perceive with the eyes
41. Actress Diana
42. Roman sandal
43. Compels
46. Dexterous
49. Encourage in wrongdoing
50. Cockeyed
51. Woven strip of fine material
54. Ecol., e.g.
57. Fastener
58. Exaggerated
60. Bird of prey
61. Basketball Hall-of-Famer Archibald
62. Egg producer
63. Prophet
64. Chemical endings
65. Revolt

DOWN
1. Great quantity
2. Dice
3. Smallest component
4. Calculus calculation: Abbr.
5. Spearlike implement
6. Arrows
7. Daughter of Zeus
8. Lubricates
9. Sham
10. Jamaican music style
11. Bacteria discovered by Theodor Escherich
12. Idle
13. Run away with a lover
18. Indian bread
23. Gaiter
25. Digital readout, for short
26. Managed care grps.
27. First-class
28. Ballet movement
29. Sharp tastes
30. Blood letters
33. Preservative
34. Bide-___
35. Transcript stats
37. Guide
38. Period of human life
39. Capricorn symbol
41. Bill of Rights subj.
42. Loud voiced person
43. Crab's claw
44. Cavalry sword
45. Native Nigerians
46. Cabbies
47. "Kate & ___"
48. Nightclub
52. "Terrible" czar
53. "La Belle et la ___"
54. Pierce with knife
55. Wax
56. Romantic interlude
59. Greeting

80

Puzzle 41

ACROSS
1. Steeple
6. Highway
10. Army N.C.O.
14. Ventilated
15. Otherwise
16. Concern
17. Pain-killers
19. Colored
20. Farewell
21. Seemingly mocking fate
22. Had too much, briefly
23. Earth sci.
24. Scarce thing
26. Not necessary (3-9)
31. Praying figure
32. Barbed comments
33. Common Market inits.
36. "Elephant Boy" boy
37. Over
39. Capital of Norway
40. 1997 U.S. Open champ
41. Elide
42. Garden products brand
43. Responsibility
46. Norse
49. Bismarck's state: Abbr.
50. Concert sites
51. Humiliated
54. ___ king
57. ___ Station
58. Recalled the past
60. Ballpark figs.
61. Nipple
62. French story
63. Mont. neighbor
64. "___, Brute!"
65. Abrupt

DOWN
1. Car from Trollhättan
2. Suggestive of pine trees
3. Requiem Mass word
4. Divinity school subj.
5. Most provocative
6. Put a new sole on
7. Lena of "Chocolat"
8. Fungal spore sacs
9. Give an account of
10. Black tourmaline
11. Meccan, e.g.
12. Hail
13. Woman's one-piece undergarment
18. Greek god of love
23. Knee
25. Walkman batteries
26. Facial feature
27. Spoken
28. Captures
29. Norse god of winds
30. 23rd letter of the Hebrew alphabet
33. Book after Neh.
34. Like some textbook publishers
35. Fowl enclosure
37. Menu option
38. Sticker
39. Ural River city
41. ___ generis
42. Cutting down
43. Danzig
44. Undisturbed
45. Capital of Yemen
46. Slangy denials
47. Black Sea port, new-style
48. Tears
52. Root vegetable
53. Amo, amas, ___
54. Rent-___
55. Chair supports
56. Chick's tail?
59. ___-Foy, Que.

Puzzle 42

ACROSS
1. Patron Saint of France
6. Cookbook abbr.
10. Fail to hit
14. Smart ___
15. Looker
16. Image of a deity
17. Puppet
19. Tyne of "Judging Amy"
20. Arafat's grp.
21. Best at putting things away
22. Indian pulses
23. Migrant farm worker
24. Conjecture or opinion
26. Lack of proper nutrition
31. Hymn
32. Departed
33. Label
36. Nautical call
37. Covered with slime
39. Huxtable boy
40. Cries of regret
41. Hawaiian feast
42. Get to know
43. Transformation of food into body tissue
46. "Dixie" composer
49. "The Turtle" poet
50. ___ Clinic
51. Counting frame
54. Mature
57. Belgian composer Jacques
58. Illuminated
60. Colour of unbleached linen
61. Kernels
62. Squeezing (out)
63. Improvised bed
64. Eye inflammation
65. Oriental peanut sauce

DOWN
1. Moist
2. Airline since 1948
3. Emperor of Rome 54-68
4. Here, elsewhere
5. Impressive
6. Sway
7. Unit of computer memory
8. Bristle
9. Make pretty
10. Refuse heap
11. State in the NW United States
12. Pertaining to the sun
13. Cunningly
18. Ravel's "Gaspard de la ___"
23. Merely
25. Torrid
26. Movie-rating org.
27. Wan
28. South-east Asian nation
29. Hipbone
30. President pro ___
33. Siamese
34. Prefix, air
35. Beethoven's birthplace
37. Withstands
38. My ___, Vietnam
39. 9th letter of the Hebrew alphabet
41. "Saving Private Ryan" craft: Abbr.
42. Birds
43. Greek god of the winds
44. As a precaution
45. Praise
46. Solidly fix in surrounding mass
47. - Polo
48. Fort ___, Fla.
52. Very dry champagne
53. Ostentatious
54. Battling
55. Actress Rowlands
56. Nervously irritable
59. Alias

Puzzle 43

ACROSS

1. Hired thugs
6. N.Y.P.D. employee
10. Animistic god or spirit
14. Maine college town
15. "The Lion King" lion
16. Nobel Prize subj.
17. Person who confers a benefit
19. South African mountain
20. Dockworker's org.
21. Simple life form
22. ___ Sea (Amu Darya's outlet)
23. Jack-in-the-pulpit, e.g.
24. Coarse-ground meal
26. Readiness
31. Tramps
32. Double curve
33. Anger
36. As soon as possible
37. Serf
39. Cain's victim
40. Cartoon canine
41. Bottom
42. Slap
43. Keyboard instruments
46. Arizona tourist locale
49. Small recess
50. European auto
51. German emperor
54. "The Simpsons" bartender
57. Girl's plaything
58. Ambitions
60. Part of a Spanish play
61. Laugh loudly
62. S-bends
63. "Heartbreak House" writer
64. Current month
65. ___ Dame

DOWN

1. Desert in E Asia
2. Baseball's Hershiser
3. A Mrs. Chaplin
4. GPS heading
5. To the extent that
6. Receipts
7. ___ the Great (boy detective)
8. Untidy person
9. Small parrot
10. Skewered meat portions
11. Bitter
12. Ethic
13. Fireplace
18. Russia/Manchuria boundary river
23. Each
25. Expert finish?
26. "___ Lap" (1983 film)
27. Fragrant flower
28. Abba of Israel
29. Apportions
30. Vietnam's ___ Dinh Diem
33. Bridge support
34. In-basket stamp: Abbr.
35. The "E" of B.P.O.E.
37. Ceremonial suicide
38. Extrasensory perception
39. Every which way
41. Prohibit
42. Make shorter
43. Empty
44. Put in
45. "Fargo" director
46. Ice-cream drinks
47. An age
48. Greek letter
52. Soon
53. "Take ___ a sign"
54. The majority
55. Unique thing
56. To be, in old Rome
59. Equal: Prefix

Puzzle 44

ACROSS
1. Void
6. Greek theaters
10. Sharp ringing sound
14. Stir
15. Make waves
16. Munich's river
17. Elusive
19. Article in Der Spiegel
20. Boardroom bigwig
21. Make tidy
22. Sprint contest
23. Time of abstinence
24. German cathedral city
26. Not redeemable
31. Impertinent
32. Young cow
33. "Kapow!"
36. Luxuriant
37. Pond scum
39. Explosive device
40. Capone and Capp
41. Actress Falco
42. Ancient Aegean land
43. Ancestors
46. Fuse pottery or glass
49. Andy's radio partner
50. 30's boxing champ Max

51. Axilla
54. Tre + tre
57. Biology lab supply
58. Visionary
60. Roman censor
61. Daybreak
62. ___-cochere (carriage entrance)
63. Heaps
64. To be, to Brutus
65. Fencing needs

DOWN
1. ___-a-brac
2. Solitary
3. Motor car
4. Code-cracking org.
5. 35th president of the U.S
6. A narcotic
7. Something owing
8. Author ___ Stanley Gardner
9. Agreeable
10. Penetrate
11. Thomas of the N.B.A.
12. Effeminate male
13. Color
18. Hereditary factor
23. Poland's Walesa
25. 1936 candidate Landon
26. Cuba, por ejemplo
27. Actor Julia

28. Moscow's land: Abbr.
29. John D. MacDonald sleuth Travis ___
30. Battery size
33. Pro ___
34. Mideast chief: Var.
35. Budding entrepreneurs, for short
37. SA capital
38. Cover
39. Employer
41. An age
42. Heavy hydrogen, e.g.
43. Marshall -, N.T. chief minister
44. U.S. gangster
45. Actor Jannings
46. Manila hemp plant
47. Bedevil
48. "Groovy!"
52. Suggestions on food labels: Abbr.
53. Street of stabling
54. Father
55. 90° from norte
56. Suffix with social
59. Republicans, for short

88

Puzzle 45

ACROSS
1. Reveals
6. Fool
10. Hindu garment
14. Capital of Ghana
15. Neighbor of Tenn.
16. Cool drinks
17. Extraordinary
19. Gds.
20. Dadaism founder
21. Felonies
22. Endure
23. Curl
24. Card game for two
26. Member of a commission
31. Cry of terror
32. Ornamental fabric
33. Fairy queen
36. Delineate
37. "Get ___!"
39. Nip
40. Speck
41. Parasitic insect
42. Iodine solution
43. Hair styling
46. Sumptuous, especially elegant
49. Chester Arthur's middle name
50. Baseball stats
51. Drew close to
54. Dockworkers'
org.
57. Ages and ages
58. Before death
60. Pond organism
61. Stupid person
62. Bob Marley fan
63. Christian name
64. Glimpse
65. Astir

DOWN
1. Vamp Theda
2. The maple
3. Dudley Do-Right's org.
4. Period of history
5. Fleshy
6. Garden pests
7. Part of a nuclear arsenal, for short
8. Man
9. State of being present
10. Asian deer
11. Serpent
12. Took examination again
13. Grenoble's department
18. Malay dagger
23. "Hurry up!"
25. Average
26. Chill
27. U.S. State
28. People in charge: Abbr.
29. Homer's epic
30. Idiot
33. Skirt coming to just below knee
34. Heaps and heaps
35. Lux. neighbor
37. Legal status of an alien
38. Celtic Neptune
39. Boatswain
41. Machine for sending documents
42. Dancer Duncan
43. Hungarian cavalryman
44. To make less dense
45. K-6: Abbr.
46. Great fear
47. Carlo Levi's "Christ Stopped at ___"
48. Language
52. 1940's-50's All-Star ___ Slaughter
53. At the apex
54. "Wishing won't make ___"
55. Mother of Apollo
56. Last of a Latin trio
59. Churchill's "so few": Abbr.

Puzzle 46

ACROSS
1. Chaplain
6. "Gil ___"
10. Disrespectful back talk
14. Soul
15. Ear part
16. Back part of the foot
17. Surgery drug
19. Like custard
20. Radiation unit
21. Shores
22. Article in Die Zeit
23. Crocodile (Colloq)
24. Government morals protector
26. Cancerous tissue treatment
31. Under
32. Bullfighter's cloak
33. Consumer protection org.
36. Gershwin biographer David
37. Untrue
39. ___-kiri
40. Cellular stuff
41. She played Glinda in "The Wiz"
42. French equivalent of the Oscar
43. Timorous
46. Artificial leg
49. A Guthrie
50. Musical instrument
51. Ex ___ (from nothing)
54. Chiang ___-shek
57. Very sweet
58. Travellers
60. "Come Back, Little Sheba" playwright
61. Big zero
62. Angry
63. Affirmative votes
64. Valley
65. Chili con ___

DOWN
1. Punnily titled 1952 quiz show "Up to ___"
2. Indian currency
3. Expired
4. Real estate ad abbr.
5. Be humiliated
6. Remove the color from
7. Profit failure
8. Not much
9. View of the sea
10. Lustrous
11. Sponsorship
12. Music, sign
13. More wily
18. Loud derisory cry
23. "Let's go!"
25. Clean air grp.
26. "Good buddy"
27. Chopped
28. Parmenides' home
29. Showy actions
30. Dorm authority figures: Abbr.
33. Strong woody fiber
34. Scottish hillside
35. Poet
37. Pretending
38. Curry of "Today"
39. Champion
41. New Guinea seaport
42. Pertaining to heat
43. Bends
44. Island in the South China Sea
45. Colleague of Dashiell
46. Lecterns
47. Deep, lustrous black
48. Overcharge
52. Emphatic type: Abbr.
53. Conceal
54. Knot in wood
55. Env. notation
56. "Amazing Grace" ending
59. Celestial altar

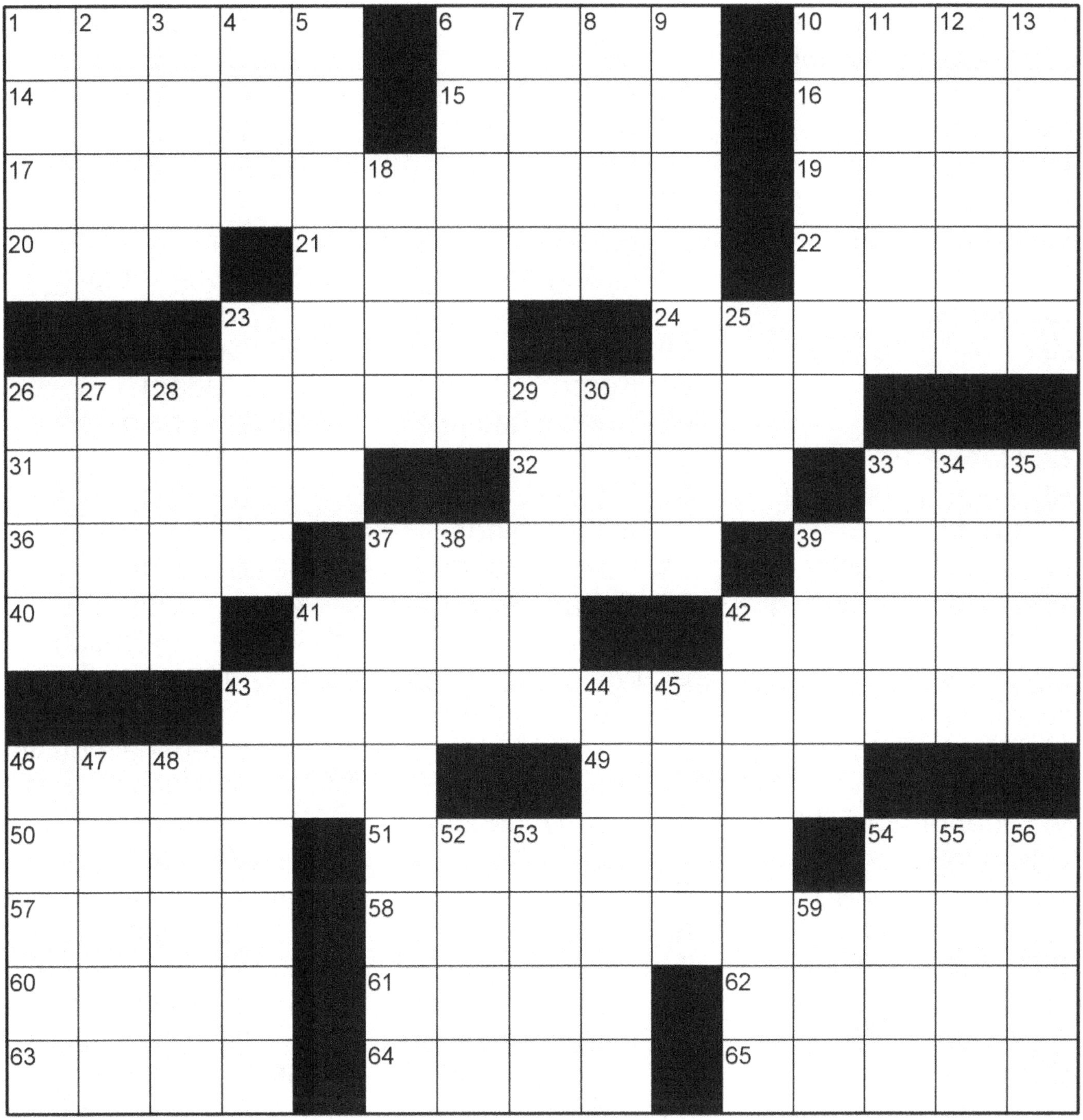
1 2 3 4 5 6 7 8 9 10 11 12 13
14 15 16
17 18 19
20 21 22
23 24 25
26 27 28 29 30
31 32 33 34 35
36 37 38 39
40 41 42
43 44 45
46 47 48 49
50 51 52 53 54 55 56
57 58 59
60 61 62
63 64 65

Puzzle 47

ACROSS

1. Ancient assembly area
6. Stringed instrument
10. "Serpico" author Peter
14. Cults
15. Scent
16. Assuming that's true
17. Grossness
19. Midday
20. "For ___ a jolly ..."
21. Revere
22. Rabbit fur
23. Contemporary of Agatha
24. Summer cooler
26. Large overstuffed sofa
31. Stops
32. Monster
33. "Monty Python" airer
36. Seat of Garfield County, Okla.
37. Daphnis's love
39. Water craft
40. J.F.K. regulators
41. Student at mixed school
42. Jester
43. Keyboard instruments
46. 3 Targe
49. Thick slice

50. Psychohistorian Seldon of Isaac Asimov's "Foundation" books
51. Birth pains
54. Alcott book "___ Boys"
57. Gardner and others
58. Giving a glassy finish to
60. Coin
61. Kemo ___
62. Convocation of witches
63. Malay dagger with a wavy blade
64. Celestial body
65. Submachine guns

DOWN

1. Author Sholem
2. "Chicago" star, 2002
3. Wood sorrels
4. A.C.L.U. concerns: Abbr.
5. Avers
6. Warmer
7. Together, in music
8. Part of verb to ride
9. First public showing
10. Ground meat
11. Astir
12. All together
13. "Crime and Punishment"

heroine
18. Small island
23. Founded: Abbr.
25. French key
26. Head cook
27. Mandlikova of tennis
28. "Last Essays of ___," 1833
29. Furls
30. "Where did ___ wrong?"
33. Dull person
34. Madam
35. Egg holders: Abbr.
37. Lacking a cord
38. With it, once
39. Small drop
41. ___ Poly
42. Heir to British throne
43. Robberies
44. Chemical cousin
45. A hint
46. Shanty
47. Vacillate
48. Khomeini, for one
52. Med school subj.
53. Small yeast cake
54. Zigzag before the wind (Yachting)
55. ___ even keel
56. Some N.C.O.'s
59. "Saving Private Ryan" craft: Abbr.

Puzzle 48

ACROSS

1. Former name of Thailand
5. Actress Gibbs
10. Calculating types
14. French wave
15. Willow
16. Italy's ___ di Como
17. Utopian
19. Wood sorrels
20. One way to see
21. Heterosexual (Colloq)
23. Env. contents
24. Crosses with loops
25. Fatal
29. ___-Ball (arcade game)
30. Ovum
33. Bandleader Skinnay ___
34. The Beatles' "___ Leaving Home"
35. Huge amounts
36. Seaward
37. Dupes
38. "___ girl!"
39. Jamaican exports
40. Magician's opening
41. Eminent
42. Classified ad abbr.
43. Not genuine: Abbr.
44. Warns
45. Boris and Natasha's boss
47. Mil. rank
48. Large bodies of water
50. Vigorous exercises
55. Intro drawing class
56. Weekly
58. Regretted
59. First name in 2000 news
60. Verne's submariner
61. Sun. talks
62. Performers
63. Yawn

DOWN

1. French silk
2. May event, for short
3. "Song of the South" song syllables
4. Flesh
5. A half
6. From Nineveh: Abbr.
7. Ritual
8. Garland
9. Slyness
10. Fabric
11. Leader
12. Food thickener
13. Just passable (2-2)
18. Lounges
22. Supplement
24. Cub leader
25. "The Wreck of the Mary ___"
26. Follow
27. Wind speed measuring instrument
28. "Buenos ___"
29. Brief
31. Reached
32. Biting insects
34. 1924 Ferber novel
35. River in central Switzerland
37. Extremely hungry
41. Dimness
43. Son of, in Arabic names
44. Protective kitchen garments
46. Incursions
47. Timber tree
48. Paddles
49. Rock's Motley ___
50. Anne Nichols hero
51. Explosive sound
52. Notion
53. Group of tents
54. ___ gin fizz
57. "Don't Bring Me Down" grp.

Puzzle 49

ACROSS
1. Cheats
5. Indian melodies
10. From a distance
14. Rich soil
15. Develop
16. Wool package
17. Insurrection
19. On the top
20. Recurring designs
21. Easily tamed birds
23. Prefix, new
24. Maj.'s superior
25. Attacks
29. Cries of surprise
30. - and outs, intricacies
33. Use
34. Bedouin
35. Largest continent
36. Nee
37. Damn
38. Anatomical canal
39. For dieters
40. Melody
41. Slight sharp sound
42. Old English letter
43. Diamond stats
44. Zodiac sign
45. ___ artery
47. New Zealand bird
48. Operated by hand
50. Past recollections
55. Like some profs.
56. By some measure
58. Stand
59. Wee
60. Bill producers
61. British tax
62. "Ditto"
63. Architect ___ van der Rohe

DOWN
1. Fastener
2. Eugene O'Neill's daughter
3. Big name in magazine publishing
4. Filth
5. Rue
6. Gland: Prefix
7. Firearms
8. N.C. State is in it
9. Appear
10. Two islands in the N Bahamas
11. Submissive to fate
12. Nautical, below
13. Gym set
18. Pertaining to the kidneys
22. Coolers, briefly
24. Capital of Tibet
25. Architectural feature
26. Egg-shaped
27. Earthy nature
28. Trigonometric function
29. Gold braid
31. Female relative
32. Chemises
34. Golden
35. Bothers
37. Occult doctrine
41. Slangy greetings
43. Creek
44. Big citrus fruit
46. Baits
47. ___ Park, N.J.
48. Ford product, briefly
49. Friend, to Françoise
50. Water filled barricade
51. Quantity of paper
52. Monetary unit of Peru
53. Salinger heroine
54. Cong. period
57. "Trust ___" (1937 hit)

Puzzle 50

ACROSS
1. Club-like weapon
5. Ales
10. Their days are numbered
14. Stickers
15. Brother of Moses
16. Prefix, sun
17. Utterly unyielding
19. Metallic element
20. Source of the quote
21. Pilots
23. Egyptian serpent
24. Giraffe-like animal
25. 4th letter of the Hebrew alphabet
29. Meat cut
30. ___ Na Na
33. Dance partner for Fred
34. Fluster
35. "The fix ___"
36. French chef's mushroom
37. Lid
38. Highland skirt
39. Dear, as a signorina
40. Military sch.
41. Rock cavity
42. Beer
43. Periods of history
44. Climbing plants
45. Fishing basket
47. Conger
48. On dry land
50. Green onion
55. ___ de soie (silk cloth)
56. Practical or strict attitude (2-8)
58. Stopper
59. Ancient Roman magistrate
60. Muslim honorific
61. Having a sound mind
62. Outmoded
63. Distribute cards

DOWN
1. New corp. hires
2. Autobahn sight
3. Crustacean
4. Salinger lass
5. Exile
6. Consume
7. Greek goddess of strife
8. 1980's White House nickname
9. More underhanded
10. Bird sound
11. Authorization
12. Drug-yielding plant
13. Ireland's ___ Fein
18. Winged
22. "At Seventeen" singer Janis
24. Seeped
25. Bangladesh's capital, old-style
26. "Let's Make ___"
27. Irish sprite
28. Zeno of ___
29. They go with the flow
31. Broom ___ (comics witch)
32. Poker stakes
34. At a focus
35. Big furniture retailer
37. Heeled over
41. Fish organs
43. Always, in verse
44. Tilted
46. Article of make-up
47. French school
48. Computer programs, for short
49. Ward of "Sisters"
50. Fit of rage
51. Metal
52. "Good Luck, Miss Wyckoff" novelist
53. Dept. of Labor arm
54. "Hud" Oscar winner
57. Room within a harem

Puzzle 51

ACROSS
1. Car since 1949
5. Loops
10. "Peter Pan" pirate
14. French military cap
15. "Tomorrow" musical
16. Granada greeting
17. Tyrannical
19. Work without ___
20. Tottering person
21. Main arteries
23. Social insect
24. Hoisted, nautically
25. Flag
29. Eager
30. Literary monogram
33. Cherubs
34. King Harald's father
35. ___ prima (painting technique)
36. Rant
37. Coeur d'___
38. God: Sp.
39. Chemical endings
40. Not masc. or fem.
41. Nancy Drew's creator
42. Small drink
43. Bickering
44. Exceed
45. "Hamlet" courtier
47. "Dilbert" cartoonist Scott Adams has one: Abbr.
48. Cloying
50. Cobweb filament
55. Mex. neighbor
56. Burdensome
58. Floating ice
59. ___-foot oil
60. Stuff
61. Almost forever
62. Relaxes
63. - Christian Andersen

DOWN
1. Slide
2. Air (prefix)
3. Footless animal
4. Tie
5. Piles of stones
6. Beginning
7. Foreword: Abbr.
8. Falsehood
9. Tranquilliser
10. Emmy-winning Lewis
11. Capital of Vermont
12. Zeno's home
13. Consumes
18. Terrors
22. W.A. river
24. Opposite of après
25. Worries
26. Mideasterner
27. Magical potion
28. Crude minerals
29. Sealskin wearer, maybe
31. Lengthwise
32. Stroll
34. Kind of acid
35. "Zip-___-Doo-Dah"
37. Sophocles tragedy
41. Russian drink
43. Prince Valiant's son
44. Dominate ones thoughts
46. Dimensions
47. Death in Venice
48. Secure
49. Alice's chronicler
50. Transcript stats
51. "Happy Birthday, Moon" author Frank
52. Oscar winner Sorvino
53. Hunter of fiction
54. Radiation dosages
57. Legume

ACROSS

1. Narrow ledge
5. Extended operatic solo
10. Gospel singer Winans
14. June 6, 1944
15. Song
16. Rat tail?
17. Boisterously wild
19. Gael
20. Consisting of metal
21. Greek island in the Aegean Sea
23. Laboratory
24. Follow, as a tip
25. Matter
29. Malay dagger with a wavy blade
30. Discount rack abbr.
33. Stare angrily
34. Top dog
35. Egyptian deity
36. Death rattle
37. Perhaps
38. Leeds's river
39. "___ Excited" (Pointer Sisters hit)
40. "___ Coming" (1969 hit)
41. Quick
42. Born
43. Envelope abbr.
44. Fix in advance
45. Start of a toast
47. Battery type
48. Tooth in front?
50. Union
55. Sainted pope called "the Great"
56. Road hugger
58. "M
59. Clarifying phrase
60. Blood type, briefly
61. Exchequer
62. Class of Indian society
63. Big mouths

DOWN

1. Real estate ad abbr.
2. Actress McClurg
3. Ecstatic
4. "___ Breckinridge"
5. Having only magnitude
6. West Indies native
7. Director Rohmer
8. Prefix, not
9. Preparation for killing algae
10. Chocolate nut
11. Very long times
12. City southwest of Bogotá
13. Editorial cartoonist Hulme
18. North of Virginia
22. Pennies: Abbr.
24. Semites
25. Smiling
26. Burning gas
27. Lies
28. Mars: Prefix
29. Enter, as data
31. Kind of show
32. Butler at Tara
34. Stops
35. Wan
37. Pertaining to meteors
41. Feeble
43. Talent
44. Roof of the mouth
46. Granddaddy of all computers
47. Crème de la crème
48. Elgar's "King ___"
49. Delicatessen
50. Fruity coolers
51. Smallest component
52. One of Columbus's ships
53. Ship's company
54. Lines of thought, for short?
57. Nabokov novel

Puzzle 53

ACROSS
1. Org. with eligibility rules
5. Greek island
10. Spanish words of agreement (2.2)
14. Goya's "Duchess of ___"
15. Ammonia derivative
16. Med school subj.
17. Australian lungfish
19. Archibald of the N.B.A.
20. Irascible
21. More crimson
23. Bullfight call
24. Thicket
25. Be innate
29. Main island of Indonesia
30. Which was to be proved
33. Cheerful
34. Destiny
35. Electrical safety device
36. Farm prefix
37. More pleasant
38. Assess
39. Beatty and Buntline
40. Large trees
41. Furnishings
42. Family

43. Towards the centre
44. Redo letter on typewriter
45. Effort
47. "For ___ a jolly ..."
48. Perches
50. Band of gems worn around neck
55. Tolkien creatures
56. Pens
58. Capital of Azerbaijan
59. Ventilate again
60. Repose
61. Otherwise
62. New England catch
63. Actress Winslet

DOWN
1. Catches
2. Tribe
3. Start of a magician's cry
4. Modern Maturity grp.
5. Word with similar meaning
6. Entertain
7. Chi follower
8. Rum
9. Pirate
10. ___ of time
11. Deficiency

12. Surfeit
13. Anatomical passage
18. Nautical, to the left
22. Clean air org.
24. Choice food
25. Dinar spender
26. Actor Bruce
27. Adversity
28. 1961 chimp in space
29. Hollowed pumpkin
31. Bar, at the bar
32. Caterpillar competitor
34. Autostrada sights
35. Worry
37. Teetotalers
41. Writing tables
43. Believer's suffix
44. Tape conversation
46. Hand out
47. Prefix, sun
48. Gown
49. Spoken
50. Tenn. neighbor
51. Skulk
52. Extent of space
53. Girdle
54. Boiardo's patron
57. Computer giant

Puzzle 54

ACROSS
1. "Hurlyburly" playwright
5. Republic in W Africa
10. French cheese
14. "Très ___!"
15. Loaded cargo
16. Long fish
17. Vacillating
19. ___ prof.
20. Aware
21. Company with a kangaroo logo
23. "Norma ___"
24. Rage
25. Hebrew prophet
29. Madam
30. "Jurassic Park" mathematician ___ Malcolm
33. Bestow
34. Secular
35. Adolescent pimples
36. Comedian Carvey
37. Pixie
38. Old Fords
39. Elvis ___ Presley
40. Tach readings
41. 1975 Pulitzer-winning critic
42. French possessive
43. Regrets
44. Knives
45. In-box contents
47. Girl (Slang)
48. Slyness
50. Shaped like a sesame seed
55. 1961 space chimp
56. Easy to reach
58. N.Y. neighbor
59. Large duck-like bird
60. "Star Wars" princess
61. Kind of shoppe
62. "Women Who Run With the Wolves" author
63. Looked over

DOWN
1. Grand slam foursome
2. Suffix with concession
3. Capital of Switzerland
4. Hydrocarbon suffixes
5. Worldwide
6. Oscar-winning Berry
7. Together, on a score
8. Seine
9. Sufficiency
10. Gambling game
11. Limited
12. "Casablanca" heroine
13. Guesses: Abbr.
18. Fathered
22. Limb
24. Carnivals
25. Pops
26. Conscious
27. One billionth of a second
28. Republic in SW Asia
29. Cripples
31. Auto pioneer Citroën
32. Nidi
34. Coat collar part
35. Jessica of "Dark Angel"
37. Fruits collectively
41. Fitzgerald and others
43. Thor Heyerdahl craft
44. Chorus section
46. Intervening
47. Large duck-like birds
48. Art ___
49. Hydroxyl compound
50. Native of Scotland
51. Long distance
52. Heed
53. Tennis star, - Natase
54. No longer living
57. Long-leaved lettuce

Puzzle 55

ACROSS
1. Fargo's state: Abbr.
5. Nobelist Bohr
10. Ices
14. Medieval chest
15. Containing iodine
16. Soft drink variety
17. Capable of being drawn back
19. Tenor in "The Flying Dutchman"
20. Shallow freight boat
21. Nebraska river
23. French pronoun
24. Lack of tone
25. Fair-haired
29. Italian currency
30. Not (prefix)
33. "A Delicate Balance" playwright
34. Bundle
35. Citrus fruit
36. Casa chamber
37. Portals
38. Once again
39. Not orig.
40. ___-doke
41. Concerning
42. A delay

43. Mountain goat
44. Exceedingly
45. Network, e.g.
47. Bleat of a sheep
48. Small bus
50. Essential amino acid
55. Busy
56. Vacillated
58. Last name in fashion
59. Daughter of one's brother or sister
60. Wheel hub
61. Sicilian resort
62. Student tables
63. Fed chairman Greenspan

DOWN
1. Police informer
2. Endure
3. Entr'___
4. Baedeker of the Baedeker travel guides
5. Designer Miller
6. Bits
7. Redact
8. "___ Abner"
9. Rods of office
10. Large body of water
11. Prospector of

1849
12. Flutter
13. Rice wine
18. Live
22. Mauna ___
24. Alvin of dance
25. Herb variety
26. South American beast
27. Sense of duty
28. Tidy
29. Rubber tree juice
31. Portents
32. Unfamiliar with
34. Bread maker
35. Narrow country road
37. Surpass
41. Benefit
43. Wrath
44. Birds of prey
46. The "I" in IV
47. Building block
48. Green stone
49. Have ___ for
50. Beats by tennis service
51. Grandmother
52. Not rom.
53. Gulf of Finland feeder
54. Paradise
57. "Sprechen ___ Deutsch?"

Puzzle 56

ACROSS
1. Rube
5. Jowl
10. Naval noncoms
14. Indolently
15. "In what way?"
16. Part of T.A.E.
17. Good-for-nothing
19. Lose water
20. Fails
21. Standards of perfection
23. Company V.I.P.
24. Door handles
25. Asian deer
29. 20th letter of the Hebrew alphabet
30. Powdery residue
33. Fish basket
34. Stigma
35. French tire
36. Freed from Cleveland
37. Cabdriver
38. Brain passage
39. Advance money
40. Galatea's love
41. ___ Novo (Benin's capital)
42. Finish
43. In ___ way
44. Gorge
45. Bequeath
47. Illustrative craft

48. Establish a plant again
50. Very quickly
55. Mideast ruler
56. Extra
58. Brown alternative
59. Singer Crystal
60. Projecting edge
61. Work units
62. "Oklahoma!" aunt
63. Scottish hills

DOWN
1. Posterior
2. ___ fixe (obsession)
3. Musical staff sign
4. Actress Sedgwick
5. Wrath
6. Bookstore section
7. Female sheep
8. Immigrant's subj.
9. Asian mink
10. "The Alienist" author Carr
11. Courteous remark
12. Egg-shaped
13. "The Odd Couple" director
18. Of a Duke
22. Scale note
24. Pavement edges

25. Climb
26. "One for My Baby" composer
27. Wandering
28. Curve
29. Violently intense
31. Handle
32. A Great Lake
34. South American parrot
35. Subatomic particle
37. Trade along the coast
41. One of the Reagans
43. Fuss
44. Volcano mouth
46. Scandinavian Fates
47. Old womanish
48. Take by force
49. Part of E.M.T.: Abbr.
50. Tennyson work
51. All-Star reliever Nen
52. Apropos of
53. First son of Adam and Eve
54. "The moan of doves in immemorial ___": Tennyson
57. Indian dish

Puzzle 57

ACROSS
1. Spacing wedge
5. Summoned
10. Throws softly
14. Robust
15. Greene of "Bonanza"
16. Chanteuse Adams
17. City on the Oka
18. "32 Flavors" singer Davis
19. Style
20. Absence of passion
22. Unpleasant
24. Certain école
25. Belong
26. Small remnant
29. Ambitions
33. Plead
36. Requiring an acid environment
40. Intestinal parts
42. Haile Selassie disciple
43. Corker
44. Alighting
47. Cambridge sch.
48. Assail
49. Prophet
51. Ostrich-like birds
55. "Get ___ of yourself!"
59. City on the Susquehanna
61. Quickly

62. Phi Delt, e.g.
63. "A Woman Called ___" (Emmy-winning TV movie)
65. Sacks
66. Lure
67. Someone ___ (not mine)
68. Double curve
69. Information
70. Grassy plain
71. Some male dolls

DOWN
1. Shallow water
2. Shrew
3. Pertaining to the ileum
4. Thawed
5. Stage show
6. Big screen letters
7. "Mr. Belvedere" co-star
8. Boredom
9. Distributed cards
10. Essential oil of lemons
11. Baseball's Blue Moon
12. Remain
13. Witness
21. Bickerer in the "Iliad"
23. Breathe with relief
27. Beige
28. Composer ___

Carlo Menotti
30. Astringent
31. Caron role
32. Short tail
33. Offers a price
34. "Night" author Wiesel
35. Romance tale
37. It ends in Oct.
38. Elevator man
39. Glass panel
41. Almond-flavored liqueur
45. Roman emperor after Galba
46. Cog
50. Antelope
52. TV actress Georgia
53. Coral island
54. Hot sauce
56. ___ orange
57. Wearer of three stars: Abbr.
58. Measures of medicine
59. Setting for Camus's "The Plague"
60. Naive person
61. El ___, Tex.
62. Law enforcement agency
64. Lair

ACROSS

1. Bozos
5. Like windows
10. Architect Mies van der ___
14. Ostrich-like bird
15. "You ___ mouthful!"
16. Ebony
17. Shed the feathers
18. According to
19. Performs
20. Mama Cass ___
22. Fined
24. Give new weapons to
25. Cleaning lady
26. Apiece
29. Firefighter Red
33. Medical suffix
36. Plastic surgery of the nose
40. F.D.R.'s Scottie
42. Angry
43. Level, in London
44. Scaring
47. +: Abbr.
48. La ___ opera house
49. Irene of "Fame"
51. Greek epic poem
55. Abreast
59. Never
61. Parting words
62. Expense
63. Skewered meat portions
65. Mrs. Dithers in "Blondie"
66. Zaire's Mobutu ___ Seko
67. Musical study piece
68. Indigo
69. Having wings
70. Was foolishly fond of
71. Future atty.'s hurdle

DOWN

1. Abalone
2. Stuck, after "in"
3. Mac
4. Irony
5. E.T.S. offering
6. Small batteries
7. East Indies palms
8. Dropsy
9. Challenged
10. North American juniper
11. Hautboy
12. Tilled
13. Abstract being
21. - Khayyam
23. Monetary unit of Iran
27. Voucher
28. Rent
30. As soon as possible
31. "Wishing won't make ___"
32. Bar selections
33. Rubs out
34. Artist Chagall
35. Others, to Ovid
37. Grandmother
38. Auricular
39. Baseball's Tony or Alejandro
41. Sparkling
45. Nimbus
46. Alum
50. Forming the apex
52. Blotted
53. Chemical prefix
54. First appearance
56. Ages
57. Papal court
58. Laud
59. Christmas
60. Bones
61. In bed
62. Civil War inits.
64. "The Sultan of Sulu" writer

Puzzle 59

ACROSS
1. Boardroom V.I.P.'s
5. Some sports cars, for short
10. Neighbor of Niger
14. Suffix with poet
15. English dramatist George
16. Pro follower
17. Roster
18. Clarinetist Shaw
19. Greek letters
20. Smart
22. Scraped
24. Ventilated
25. Cotton thread used for hosiery
26. Former coin of Spain
29. Actress MacDowell
33. Wee, to Burns
36. Doctrine of a Catholic church
40. Composer Schifrin
42. Botch
43. Yellow cheese coated with red wax
44. Terms
47. River to the Volga
48. Electrical rectifier
49. Measure out
51. Eskimo dwelling
55. Noted blind mathematician
59. Incense burner
61. Salad herb
62. Mountain lion
63. On fire
65. Off-Broadway theater award
66. ___ Fox
67. Greet and seat
68. Abbr. after many a general's name
69. Ethereal
70. Corneous
71. Woe is me

DOWN
1. About (Approximate date)
2. Dangerous bacteria
3. Horse opera
4. Worked hard
5. On ___ (equipotent)
6. Celtic sea god
7. Kind of position
8. Person used as one's excuse
9. Prophets
10. Belief
11. Detest
12. Just slightly
13. "___ Kapital"
21. Cabinet dept.
23. Part of a court game name
27. Butts
28. "Miss ___ Regrets"
30. Lover of Aeneas
31. Author Dinesen
32. Austen heroine
33. Sledge
34. Long, for short
35. Bowser's bowlful
37. Fu-___ (legendary Chinese sage)
38. Baseball's Blue Moon
39. Solitary
41. Commonplace
45. Lines of thought, for short?
46. Submachine gun
50. Author Welty
52. Dog's lead
53. Gluck's "___ ed Euridice"
54. Willow
56. Defame
57. "Don't Cry for Me, Argentina" musical
58. Marsh plants
59. Remedy
60. Part of E.M.T.: Abbr.
61. Counting-out word
62. Alley org.
64. "Oysters ___ season"

Puzzle 59

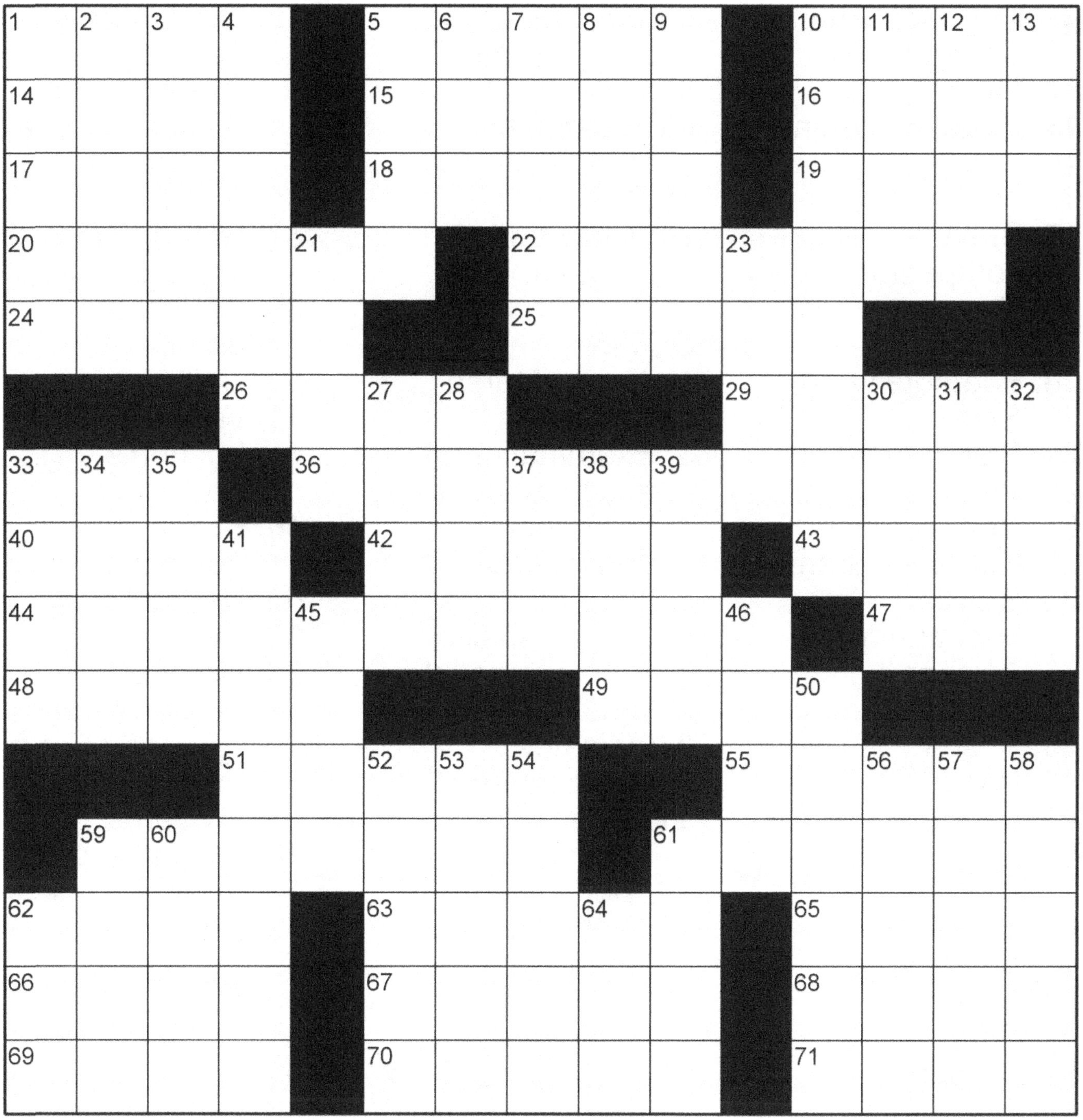

Puzzle 60

ACROSS

1. Scholastic sports grp.
5. Watered garden
10. Cook in oven
14. Morose
15. Papal vestment
16. Take ___ view of
17. BMW competitor
18. Napery
19. Flows
20. Footnote word
22. Stated
24. Blender maker
25. Very, in music
26. Neb. neighbor
29. Euripides drama
33. Russian community
36. Arranged alphabetically
40. At sea
42. Irritable
43. Sauce
44. Huge, ponderous, clumsy
47. Meadow
48. Saline
49. Scorch
51. Bordered
55. Attain
59. Accept
61. Veteran
62. Madison

Avenue award
63. Cries for attention
65. Brother of Fidel
66. "___, Brute?"
67. Rituals
68. Beaten by tennis service
69. Girl
70. Chowderhead
71. Obtains

DOWN

1. Author Marsh
2. Cudgels
3. Examination of account books
4. Ammonia derivatives
5. Ilex
6. "... ___ shall die"
7. Arabian capital
8. Hgts.
9. Indicates
10. Stockades
11. Musical direction
12. Benevolent
13. Printer's measures
21. Mother of the Valkyries
23. "___ Lama Ding Dong" (1961 hit)
27. Start of an incantation
28. Shakespearean

actor Edmund
30. Face
31. Relaxation
32. Looped handle
33. Fannie ___ (securities)
34. Madonna's "La ___ Bonita"
35. Spool
37. Hrs. on the 90th meridian
38. Christian denom.
39. Unit of force
41. Wingless
45. London's ___ Park
46. British nobleman
50. Re-haul
52. Cogs
53. Moral code
54. "A merry heart ___ good like a medicine": Proverbs
56. With speed
57. Vinegar bottle
58. Retains
59. ___ Vista
60. Skedaddles
61. ___ buco
62. Animation frame
64. 13th letter of the Hebrew alphabet

Puzzle 61

ACROSS
1. Attention
5. Humiliate
10. Eating implement
14. Author Jorge ___ Borges
15. ___ the Barbarian
16. Adjoin
17. One of the Aleutians
18. Articles
19. Something that is lost
20. Felt sympathy for
22. An inspection
24. Join lines
25. Baseball Hall-of-Famer Combs
26. Platte River tribe
29. "___ Frome"
33. Weir
36. Over
40. Parmenides' home
42. "It's ___ against time"
43. Potpourri
44. Rank of a cardinal
47. Wine: Prefix
48. Lubricated
49. Neighbor of Minn.
51. Poetic
55. Puerto ___
59. Become aware
61. Ideals
62. French novelist Pierre
63. "WarGames" org.
65. "Gil ___"
66. Founded: Abbr.
67. Soil
68. Turturro of "The Sopranos"
69. "Got it"
70. Fertile desert spots
71. Jail

DOWN
1. Applauds
2. War hero Murphy
3. Calf catcher
4. Arctic native
5. Sour
6. Fly larva
7. Anoint
8. South Pacific Islands
9. David of CNN
10. Forced high notes
11. Musical instrument
12. Stratagem
13. Gold units: Abbr.
21. "Salus populi suprema lex ___" (Missouri's motto)
23. "Fish Magic" painter
27. ___ empty stomach
28. "Buona ___" (Italian greeting)
30. Hawaii County's seat
31. Foreign pen pal
32. Inert gaseous element
33. Art ___
34. Asia's Trans ___ mountains
35. Blackbird
37. - de mer, seasickness
38. Wood sorrels
39. Abbr. after many a general's name
41. Capital of South Australia
45. Tranquil scene
46. Wyatt -
50. Knapsack
52. Fab Four member
53. Capri, e.g.
54. Roman goddess of agriculture
56. Lashes
57. Brazilian novelist Jorge
58. Of the nose
59. Antarctic explorer
60. Suffix, diminutive
61. Poems
62. Wreath of flowers
64. Marge's father-in-law on "The Simpsons"

1	2	3	4		5	6	7	8	9		10	11	12	13
14					15						16			
17					18						19			
20				21			22			23				
24						25								
			26		27	28				29		30	31	32
33	34	35		36			37	38	39					
40			41		42						43			
44				45					46			47		
48								49			50			
			51		52	53	54			55		56	57	58
	59	60							61					
62					63		64			65				
66					67					68				
69					70					71				

123

Puzzle 62

ACROSS
1. Brick carriers
5. Vampire
10. Titicaca, por ejemplo
14. Fencing sword
15. Bottomless gulf
16. Image
17. Whimper
18. Explode
19. Electrical units
20. Grooms oneself
22. Ruled
24. Decline
25. Person hiring
26. Modern Maturity org.
29. Alamogordo's county
33. Scale notes
36. Pertaining to horology
40. Notion
42. Race of Norse gods
43. Half burnt coal
44. The act of forbidding
47. "___ Girls"
48. Big Bertha's birthplace
49. "Moby-Dick" captain
51. Move to music
55. Yemen's capital
59. Oil seed
61. Be present at
62. Levee
63. First letter of the Hebrew alphabet
65. Clock pointer
66. Designer for Jackie
67. Language
68. Airline to Israel
69. Middle: Prefix
70. Saucy
71. Russo of "Get Shorty"

DOWN
1. Fibrous plants
2. Musical drama
3. Hero of 1898
4. One-named Tejano singer
5. Bell ___
6. ___ Simbel, Egypt
7. Aromatic gum used in making incense
8. Japanese immigrant
9. Moving about
10. Living in the open water
11. Continuous dull pain
12. Benevolent
13. Switch positions
21. Ark builder
23. An earth sci.
27. Thoroughfare
28. Sentence part: Abbr.
30. E.P.A. concern: Abbr.
31. Garden tool
32. Arena shouts
33. Flute
34. Bothers
35. Philly team
37. Mama bear, in Madrid
38. Director Wertmuller
39. Seating sect.
41. Companion of Daniel
45. Much may follow it
46. The Orient
50. Swimmer
52. Actress Patricia et al.
53. Salsa singer Cruz
54. Paradises
56. Football Hall-of-Famer Greasy ___
57. Boutros-Ghali's successor
58. Muddle
59. Singer Lovett
60. Alibi ___ (excuse makers)
61. Nautical call
62. Benedictine monk's title
64. Some film ratings

Puzzle 63

ACROSS
1. Broccoli ___ (leafy vegetable)
5. Book before Nahum
10. Actor Jannings
14. In bed
15. Mote
16. Baby's first word
17. Adriatic port
18. Actress Shearer
19. Broadway star Verdon
20. Summer cooler
22. Amasses
24. Item from which age is determined
25. Behind
26. Tells on
29. Heaps
33. Female deer
36. Pertaining to socialism
40. Big furniture retailer
42. Cost
43. Dame - Everage, Humphries' character
44. Doubtful
47. Line part: Abbr.
48. "___ bleu!"
49. Drag logs
51. Greek writer of fables
55. Breaks suddenly
59. Ribbed
61. Nuclear
62. Legal scholar Guinier
63. Some stars
65. Soybean paste
66. Tel ___
67. Dinar spender
68. "Beetle Bailey" dog
69. Allot
70. "A Tree Grows in Brooklyn" family name
71. Russian no

DOWN
1. Frenzied
2. Manila hemp plant
3. Tam
4. Redacted
5. Supernatural power
6. "Am ___ blame?"
7. Welsh dog
8. Capital of Jordan
9. Marriott rival
10. Sideways
11. Bryn ___
12. Ancient Roman days
13. PC linkup
21. Greek god of love
23. American Indian
27. Drill
28. Swindle
30. Old Fords
31. German article
32. Heroin
33. Immerses
34. Gumbo ingredient
35. Fair-hiring org.
37. ___ flash
38. Lawyers: Abbr.
39. Cut of meat
41. Tending to abrade
45. English court
46. Prehistoric sepulchral tomb
50. Raised part of a sundial
52. Polio vaccine developer
53. Alamogordo's county
54. Flower part
56. Friendship
57. Ski course
58. Go swiftly
59. Hollow in the earth
60. "Get ___!"
61. Abecedary link
62. Thrash
64. Alicia of "Falcon Crest"

127

Puzzle 64

ACROSS

1. Enlivens, with "up"
5. 18th letter of the Greek alphabet
10. Haul
14. Indian nursemaid
15. Gave hints
16. Geraldine Chaplin's mother
17. Winter comment
18. Stage whisper
19. First name in linguistics
20. Preference
22. Bows
24. Pope's cape
25. Choose
26. Lubricate
29. Actor Quinn
33. C.E.O.'s degree
36. Rebirth
40. Nobleman
42. Negatively charged ion
43. Gravel
44. Speech sound
47. ___ power
48. Short story
49. English college
51. Lakes
55. Scores
59. Title for a retired professor, maybe
61. Composer Prokofiev
62. Latin 101 verb
63. "Cheers" barmaid
65. "If He Walked Into My Life" musical
66. Nagy of Hungary
67. Minor oath
68. Immensely
69. Antlered beast
70. Thick
71. Actress Olin

DOWN

1. Artist Picasso
2. Monetary unit of Iceland
3. Anorak
4. Strident
5. Heroin
6. Parisian pronoun
7. Semblance
8. Award of honour
9. Dancer Astaire
10. Giving
11. Chamber
12. Literary olios
13. Leg
21. Prefix with -itis
23. Rent-___
27. Necklace component
28. Deutsche article
30. Mend socks
31. Fighting
32. Neighbor of Ger.
33. M.'s counterpart
34. Large snakes
35. Wall St. figures
37. A fool
38. Bird shelter
39. Med. sch. course
41. Distance across a circle
45. ___ and terminer
46. Booth
50. Usual
52. Like some potatoes
53. French story
54. It's a wrap
56. Gemstone
57. Citrus fruit
58. City near Florence
59. Noted plus-size model
60. Female horse
61. MS. enclosure
62. Assist
64. Mormons, initially

Puzzle 65

ACROSS
1. ___ vu
5. Portents
10. Metal dross
14. Shakespeare's river
15. Register
16. Powerful D.C. lobby
17. Café au ___
18. Its capital is St.-Étienne
19. Crazy
20. Fuse pottery or glass
22. Female ruler of an empire
24. Point in question
25. Jazz pianist Hines
26. Sentence part: Abbr.
29. Grew less
33. Brain scan, for short
36. Creative ability
40. Vigor
42. "Lorna ___"
43. McGregor of "Trainspotting"
44. They're loaded
47. Malt beverage
48. Glide along smoothly
49. Vended
51. Efface
55. Seed coverings
59. Instructs
61. Loss of volition
62. Way out
63. Trench
65. Dent
66. Sitarist Shankar
67. Cub leader
68. Greek goddess of the earth
69. Latin 101 verb
70. Nuzzles
71. Whirlpool

DOWN
1. ___ Lama
2. Olympic swimmer Janet
3. Connects
4. Pay
5. Vend
6. Daughter of Cadmus
7. Woe
8. Bellini opera
9. Dozed off
10. Suitable for sale
11. South-east Asian nation
12. Bows
13. Mail place: Abbr.
21. Air (prefix)
23. Ostrichlike bird
27. "Das Lied von der ___"
28. Singer Celine
30. Japan's largest lake
31. Bibliography abbr.
32. Unit of force
33. Wanes
34. Tenor in "The Flying Dutchman"
35. Prefix with byte
37. Deity
38. Chemical suffixes
39. Fiddling Roman emperor
41. Inflammation of bone
45. B'way showing
46. Thick slice
50. Do hard work
52. Actor Quinn
53. Watch word
54. Adlai's 1956 running mate
56. Homer's epic
57. Ceiled
58. Oriental peanut sauce
59. Test
60. Prima donna
61. Cries of discovery
62. An age
64. Diminutive suffix

Puzzle 66

ACROSS
1. Outbuilding
5. Hidden store
10. Diamond stats
14. Long distance
15. Plant insect
16. Relaxation
17. Seed covering
18. Back portions of feet
19. Ocean craft
20. Resembling cedar
22. Draws forth
24. Nancy Drew's creator
25. Pretentious sort
26. Hautboy
29. Chap
33. ___ alai
36. Self-confident
40. Blunders
42. Alpine river
43. Supernatural force
44. Extending to the floor
47. Diddley and Derek
48. Hot chocolate?
49. Expressed surprise
51. Worship
55. Halogen element
59. Religious festival
61. Secrets
62. Actress Taylor
63. Sen. Hatch
65. Not orig.
66. Work without ___ (be daring)
67. Isabella, por ejemplo
68. Booth
69. Nervous
70. Villeins
71. Baseballer Slaughter

DOWN
1. Hit
2. Person hiring
3. Slur over
4. Presidential middle name
5. "High Hopes" lyricist
6. Primate
7. Chirp
8. Small mountains
9. "Ah, Wilderness!" mother
10. Remainder
11. Monetary unit of Thailand
12. Egyptian goddess of fertility
13. Equinox mo.
21. Civil War side
23. Young scouts
27. Eye, at the Eiffel Tower
28. Otherwise
30. Crustacean
31. Game of chance
32. Harem rooms
33. Bridges in Hollywood
34. A Guthrie
35. Metallic element
37. Marsh
38. Jason's ship
39. Third son of Adam
41. Fellowship
45. New York's Giuliani
46. Inheritor
50. Tame
52. Frankincense and myrrh, but not gold
53. Kind of show
54. Monetary unit of Iceland
56. Pythias's friend
57. Architect Jones
58. Buttocks
59. Posterior
60. Couturier Cassini
61. Literary collections
62. New Guinea seaport
64. Like Beethoven's "Pastoral" Symphony

133

Puzzle 67

ACROSS
1. Leg joints
6. Grew less
11. Monetary unit of Vietnam
14. Ancient Greek colony
15. "All in the Family" spinoff
16. Gray of "Gray's Manual of Botany"
17. Brave
19. All-natural food no-no
20. Surgery sites, for short
21. Rent-a-car company
22. Skin flicks
24. Asian sea name
25. Maj.'s superior
26. Maxima maker
29. Violent criticism
32. Fatty liquid
33. Impudent children
34. Mire
35. City on the Rhine
36. "Mr. Belvedere" actress Graff
37. Clothesline clips
38. Alfonso XIII's queen
39. Maxim
40. College in Atherton, California
41. Tardiness
43. Vanquished
44. Weight measure
45. Surety
46. Tun
48. Folk singer Guthrie
49. New Guinea seaport
52. Here, in France
53. Pining
56. ___ dare
57. Farsi speaker
58. Poetic name for Ireland
59. Congeal
60. Recorded item of debt
61. Portable chair

DOWN
1. Prefix, thousand
2. Film ___
3. Baseballer Slaughter
4. Strauss's "___ Heldenleben"
5. Dry
6. Internet messages
7. Prohibits
8. However
9. Toothless
10. Subtracts
11. Clothing
12. "But, ___ was ambitious, I slew him": Brutus
13. Breakfast cereals
18. Politico Bayh
23. Beetle
24. A ___ apple
25. Climbing vine
26. Prize named after inventor of dynamite
27. Massey of "Balalaika"
28. Consisting of senators
29. Lees
30. Brass wind instrument
31. Pelé's real first name
33. World-weary
36. "My stars!"
37. Resound
39. Earthworm
40. Understatement
42. Part of E.E.C.: Abbr.
43. Indonesian resort island
45. Rumor
46. Bookstore sect.
47. Skin eruption
48. Lambs: Lat.
49. Prevaricated
50. Old Indian coin
51. Richard of "A Summer Place"
54. Arrest
55. Charlemagne's realm: Abbr.

Puzzle 68

ACROSS
1. Dog
6. "___ Majesty's Secret Service"
11. Step in ballet
14. Habituate
15. Two-time U.S. Open winner Fraser
16. Doc bloc
17. Bestowed citizenship upon
19. Flax ball
20. Opposite of a ques.
21. A legume
22. Sounds of tired joints
24. Mother of Jesus
25. Ever
26. Study of eggs
29. Openings
32. Elegance
33. Automation
34. Genetic info carrier
35. Tall and thin
36. Chief island of the Philippines
37. Young horse
38. J.F.K. posting: Abbr.
39. Justice Ruth ___ Ginsburg
40. ___ del Sol
41. Reacts

43. Pursued
44. Cheerful
45. Verse
46. Starbucks order
48. Papal edict
49. China's Chou En-___
52. Knock with knuckles
53. Resembling a tree in size
56. Period of human life
57. Knot
58. Suffix, diminutives
59. ___-relief
60. Old laborers
61. Dilettantish

DOWN
1. ___ colada
2. ___ even keel
3. Avenues of escape
4. French vineyard
5. Nonwoody vegetation
6. It's a relief
7. Teutonic turndown
8. Owns
9. Ballot
10. Rewrite
11. Cross with three horizontal crosspieces

12. Frenziedly
13. "Je ne ___ quoi"
18. Ethereal
23. Biblical high priest
24. Deride
25. Bower
26. Leerer
27. Make a speech
28. Scenic paintings
29. Seeps
30. Related on the mother's side
31. Cold meal
33. Reddish
36. Lights
37. Froth
39. Enslavement
40. Manhattan neighborhood
42. Kitchen utensil
43. "Unforgettable" singer
45. Knitting stitches
46. Clutch
47. Hindu music
48. Drill
49. Baltic native
50. Hydrocarbon suffixes
51. ___-bitsy
54. Prohibit
55. Bull's-eye: Abbr.

136

Puzzle 69

ACROSS
1. Bangladesh's capital, old-style
6. Director Kurosawa
11. Tarzan creator's monogram
14. Moslem religion
15. Consumed
16. Ed.'s request
17. City treasurer
19. Letter abbr.
20. Understanding
21. French friend
22. Culpabilities
24. Fever
25. Knowledge gained through meditation
26. Rush-like plants
29. Roof linings
32. Copycats
33. Grandmothers
34. Malt beverage
35. Hacking tool
36. Fork
37. Cartoon canine
38. Dutch city
39. Machine-guns
40. Ceaselessly
41. Sovereignty
43. Plumes
44. Fragrance
45. Cushions
46. Space rock
48. Hungarian sheepdog
49. CD predecessors
52. Clandestine maritime org.
53. Theorist
56. Prefix with meter
57. ___ Park, Colo.
58. Anouk of "La Dolce Vita"
59. Cartoon dog
60. Robert Frost farm site
61. Bridges in movies

DOWN
1. Detective (Colloq)
2. "Hard Road to Glory" author
3. Family
4. Eccentric wheel
5. Winding
6. Lofty nest
7. Cabbagelike plant
8. "Give ___ rest!"
9. Ruling
10. Yearly publications
11. Pathways by the sea
12. Engrossed
13. 1940's first lady
18. Flightless flock
23. Magician's name ending
24. Prefix with biology
25. Levis
26. Cavalry sword
27. Lyric poem
28. A group of elected representatives
29. Mate
30. Gleam
31. Sows
33. "On the Record" host Van Susteren
36. Primula
37. Single items
39. Full of life
40. Pertaining to an order
42. Part of verb to be
43. Colombian city
45. Obese
46. Anchor vessel
47. "Momo" author Michael
48. Wing: Prefix
49. Limousine (Colloq)
50. Victim
51. Propagative part of a plant
54. Cir. midpoint
55. Sicken

ACROSS

1. Quick sharp sound
6. Gettysburg commander
11. ___ diet
14. Singer Gorme
15. Pitcher, of a sort
16. Average
17. Altering
19. Brit. recording giant
20. Cousin of -trix
21. African river
22. Hummed
24. Actress Lamarr
25. Sweeping tool
26. Neighbor of Namibia
29. Rubescent
32. Venomous lizards
33. Staff leaders
34. Cultural org.
35. Growl
36. Tribe ruler
37. Dutch cheese
38. One of the Cyclades
39. Extremely
40. Designer Simpson
41. Put in bondage
43. Groups of lions
44. Vacillate
45. Father
46. Consider
48. Japanese syllabic script
49. Hawaiian acacia
52. French, water
53. Romantic tendency
56. Checkup sounds
57. Teething biscuits
58. Farm birds
59. Owing
60. Short literary composition
61. Observatory observations

DOWN

1. Wax
2. Strong cleaners
3. Nabokov heroine and others
4. Geom. figure
5. Edible parts of nuts
6. Masculine
7. Brink
8. "___ dreaming?"
9. Dead skin found in hair
10. Absorb
11. Impartial
12. Title
13. Parched
18. Slave girl of opera
23. Exclamation of wonder
24. Rime
25. Lose blood
26. Longhorn rival
27. Sheer fabric
28. Greenhouse
29. Sightless
30. Writer Zora ___ Hurston
31. Sporting events
33. Applaud
36. Eagerly desirous
37. Emmy winner Falco
39. Ancient Spanish kingdom
40. Censure
42. "Mighty ___ a Rose"
43. Confined
45. Flower
46. Heavy metal
47. Island of Hawaii
48. New Zealand parrot
49. Capital of the Ukraine
50. Greek peak
51. Cathy ___, "East of Eden" wife
54. Ed.'s pile
55. Corp. bigwig

Puzzle 71

ACROSS
1. Lecture follow-up
6. Giraffe-like animal
11. Mail abbr.
14. Asunder
15. Showed film again
16. Cathedral city
17. Harmoniously fitting in
19. Actress, - West
20. Gelid
21. For one
22. Sweeping implements
24. King of the beasts
25. Plait
26. Lengths of links
29. Having no roots
32. Luau dances
33. "Iceland" star
34. Sheltered side
35. Islamic chieftain
36. 3rd letter of the Hebrew alphabet
37. Aquatic plant
38. Eccentric shaft
39. A rich tapestry
40. Alaskan islander
41. Submerged up to the knees
43. Cutting edges
44. Titled
45. "The Laughing Cavalier" artist
46. ___ Lindgren, creator of Pippi Longstocking
48. Yahoo
49. ___ Khan
52. Color TV pioneer
53. The stiffening of a body after death (5.5)
56. Spoil
57. Audibly
58. Large cats
59. "Once in Love With ___"
60. Old "Hollywood Squares" regular
61. Filmdom's Mr. Chips

DOWN
1. Muslim judge
2. Part of the Bible: Abbr.
3. Marine defence unit
4. "___ Day" (1993 rap hit)
5. Achieves
6. The Hunter
7. Large seaweed
8. "Exodus" hero
9. Brown, in a way
10. Ungrateful person
11. Made into an improved form
12. Drumbeat
13. Stains
18. Mil. addresses
23. Lubricant
24. Fibber
25. Skeleton
26. Inquire into
27. Man's race
28. Nutritive
29. Rechart
30. Smooth transition
31. Chairs
33. Rented
36. Ravenously
37. Exclamation to express sorrow
39. Commander in chief of a fleet
40. In sum
42. Organ of hearing
43. Children's book author
45. Multitude
46. First word of the "Aeneid"
47. Confidence trick
48. Noisy
49. Like ___ of bricks
50. "Sesame Street" veterinarian
51. Aide: Abbr.
54. Geometry suffix
55. - de Janeiro

Puzzle 72

ACROSS

1. "Dallas" matriarch
6. Sorbonne, e.g.
11. Actress Benaderet
14. English poet
15. Font
16. Communication for the deaf: Abbr.
17. Transuranic element
19. Cracker biscuit
20. Father
21. Lukas of "Witness"
22. Commotion
24. Amerada ___ (Fortune 500 company)
25. The sesame plant
26. Silly
29. Mourned
32. Inclined trough
33. Persian fairies
34. Dude
35. Coarse file
36. A Gabor sister
37. Enticement
38. Halifax clock setting: Abbr.
39. Fathers
40. Swindle
41. Pertaining to germs
43. Expense
44. Synthetic fabric
45. Living units: Abbr.
46. Saline marsh
48. Bloodsucking insect
49. Cooler
52. Economic stat.
53. Collapse of the lungs
56. ___ rule
57. Tree
58. Leave of absence
59. Chihuahua on TV
60. Burst forth
61. Sea mammals

DOWN

1. Barely managed, with "out"
2. Movie princess
3. Come to ground
4. Sexless things
5. Artsy one
6. Sewing machine inventor Howe
7. Metal containers
8. Duct opening?
9. Cancer of the bone marrow
10. Fine furs
11. Court game
12. Son of Isaac and Rebekah
13. Cockeyed
18. Simple
23. "This is ___"
24. URL starter
25. Poets
26. Thin person
27. Pursue
28. Of our country
29. Juridical
30. "All My Children" vixen
31. Crazy
33. Pertaining to the pope
36. Cannibal
37. Objections
39. Light sailing ship
40. Changes
42. Noninvasive diagnostic procedure, for short
43. Oil cartel
45. Vigilant
46. Mark left by a healed wound
47. Church recess
48. A fold
49. Seaward
50. Clock face
51. Ballpark figs.
54. Dean's e-mail address ender
55. Chop

ACROSS
1. Spoke (up)
6. Actress Samantha
11. Ethnic telecaster
14. Egg-shaped
15. To haul with tackle
16. Cloak-and-dagger org.
17. Licentiously
19. Candy striper's coworkers: Abbr.
20. Explorer Johnson
21. Insect feeler
22. Strong forward rush
24. Greek letter
25. Make into an act
26. Comedienne Boosler
29. Headache
32. Spleens
33. Surfer wannabe
34. Part of U.S.N.A.: Abbr.
35. French chef's mushroom
36. Stupid people
37. Pit
38. Help wanted abbr.
39. Headdress of a bishop
40. Leper
41. Made noble
43. Assimilate
44. Dandruff
45. Donkey
46. Great one?
48. Bird of prey
49. "Who, me?"
52. "Yo te ___"
53. Desertion
56. Ballpoint biro
57. Backs of necks
58. Bird of prey
59. "A rat!"
60. Wading bird
61. Carts

DOWN
1. Equestrian sport
2. "A Little Bitty Tear" singer, 1962
3. Large almost tailless rodent
4. Biblical suffix
5. Intensifies
6. African virus
7. Ascend
8. Astronaut Grissom
9. Provided that
10. Name given to the fox
11. Examine minutely
12. Receptacles
13. Broad ribbon
18. Charge per unit
23. Company with a dog in its logo
24. Unit of computer memory
25. Downy duck
26. Master of ceremonies
27. Rest atop
28. Climbers staff
29. Sulked
30. Grandmothers
31. Turn inside out
33. Pub
36. Small bag for carrying personal items
37. Magician
39. Capital of Swaziland
40. Compared
42. It turns out Its.
43. Inflict upon
45. Middle
46. Kotter of "Welcome Back, Kotter"
47. French girlfriend
48. Leg joint
49. Prefix, large
50. Solely
51. Residents: Suffix
54. Abbr. in car ads
55. Impair

146

Puzzle 74

ACROSS

1. See red
6. City in North Rhine-Westphalia
11. Consumer protection org.
14. Graff of "Mr. Belvedere"
15. Bel ___
16. Sin
17. Kill
19. Freelancer's enc.
20. Carrier to Oslo
21. Bad: Prefix
22. Redacted
24. Civil War side
25. Prison rooms
26. Salt solution
29. Camel driver
32. African antelope
33. Prospered
34. Asian language
35. Pack of cards
36. Languished
37. Ingrid's "Casablanca" role
38. Day before
39. Planet's path
40. Avarice
41. Tape again
43. Protects
44. Playing marble
45. Bread rolls
46. Broadway opening
48. "___ Well That Ends Well"
49. Wane
52. ___ alai
53. Abnormal fear of crowds
56. That girl in "That Girl"
57. Distance downwards
58. Collectively
59. Coffee order: Abbr.
60. Donkeys
61. Jury

DOWN

1. Prejudice
2. Actress Lanchester
3. Untidy state
4. "___ Ng" (They Might Be Giants song)
5. Come down
6. Heroic tales
7. Not loco
8. Ocean
9. Revered
10. Razzed
11. Kind of list
12. Highlands hillside
13. Reared
18. Kemo ___
23. Sick
24. Skating area
25. Mark of omission
26. Exodus commemoration
27. Advil alternative
28. Tearing
29. Member of the dog family
30. Relaxed
31. Thoroughfares
33. Filament
36. Mentees
37. Nest eggs, for short
39. Source of "The True North strong and free!"
40. Armed helicopter
42. Self-esteem
43. Swallow
45. Ennui, with "the"
46. Slightly open
47. Rattan
48. Johnson of "Laugh-In"
49. Israel's Abba
50. Gall
51. Formal dance
54. Operations (colloq)
55. ___ hunch

ACROSS
1. Clique
6. The Joads, e.g.
11. "Nova" network
14. Vinegar: Prefix
15. ___-car
16. Bond rating
17. Silly person
19. Charleson of "Chariots of Fire"
20. Old letter
21. Reclined
22. Danish city that's the birthplace of Hans Christian Andersen
24. Kiln for drying hops
25. Serve as a press agent
26. Recollection
29. Customary eating hour
32. Antelope
33. Moues
34. Count Basie's "___ Darlin'"
35. Neighbor of Mont.
36. Avoid
37. "___ want for Christmas ..."
38. Calendar abbr.
39. Dye-yielding shrubs
40. General assemblies
41. Embellished
43. Key personnel
44. Anchors vessel
45. ___ fide (in bad faith)
46. Theater district
48. Dear, as a signorina
49. ___ good deed
52. Mork's planet
53. Uncontrolled
56. Shelter
57. Bacteria discovered by Theodor Escherich
58. "Family Ties" mom
59. New Deal pres.
60. Poem
61. MS. enclosures

DOWN
1. Concern
2. Part of U.S.N.A.: Abbr.
3. 2nd letter of the Hebrew alphabet
4. A.B.A. member: Abbr.
5. Wycliffe disciple
6. Regular course
7. "Show Boat" composer
8. "___ pig's eye!"
9. Drain of color
10. Types of footwear
11. Analgesic
12. Farm calls
13. Sensible
18. Not difficult
23. Outer: Prefix
24. Mrs. Chaplin
25. Ongoing hostilities
26. Gettysburg general
27. 1990's sitcom
28. Person who arranges marriages
29. Mildew
30. Pooh's creator
31. Walt Disney's middle name
33. Works at
36. Advance beyond proper limits
37. No clue
39. An additional one
40. Regal residences
42. Earthlink competitor
43. Vehicles
45. Mrs. Eisenhower
46. Massage deeply
47. Angered
48. Coal dust
49. Prohibitionists
50. Yorkshire river
51. City on the Skunk
54. - Rene. Mo
55. ___ maison (indoors): Fr.

Puzzle 75

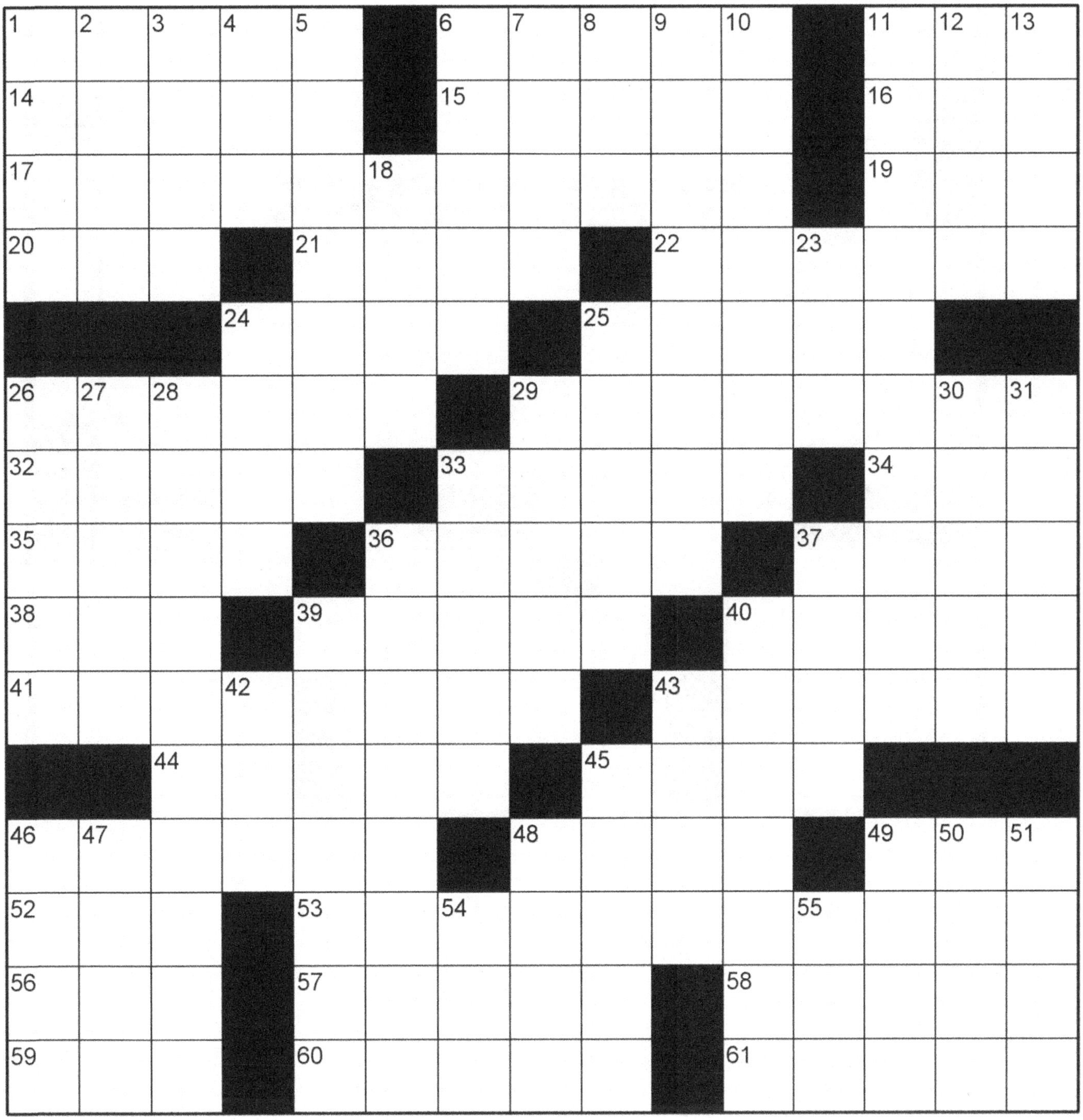

Answer 1

```
HARK  RAPID  ALOE
ILIE  IMINE  REAL
EVANESCENT   MASK
SALTLESS   ECARTE
   URN    ISIN
   LOCO  CONTAINED
BARKY  ORFEO   IBO
IVEY  NICAD   ITEM
DEO  LILAC   ISERE
ESSAYTEST  SORT
   HERD   COG
ARIOSO  SLALOMED
SHOR  GETUPANDGO
PENS  ENATE  ASIS
SASE  NOTER  LESS
```

Answer 2

```
BAER  UTICA  ATTA
ENNA  RODIN  CHOW
BIODEGRADE   CEDE
ENLIVENS   UPENDS
   SAD   PREP
   BOSN  CLAYSTONE
SEGOS  LASSO   RAS
ITIN  SEISM   FACT
MAV  AMATI   MUNRO
PSEUDONYM   INGE
   PUTS   ENC
TEMPEH  MANITOBA
BARI  ECONOMICAL
ASIS  RUNIC  OTHO
RESH  SLOSH  NAST
```

Answer 3

```
HOLD  ONEND  SGTS
YEAR  MAMIE  TARE
DIVINITIES   ROUE
ELEVATOR   COILED
   EMS   PERK
   HOWE  ORANGEMAN
GOMAD  ROWDY   AVA
UREY  ADDIS   GNAR
MSG  DRAIN   MEANY
SEAFARING   INST
   ALAN   ETD
BURDEN  RETRACTS
ETUI  GEOTHERMAL
SINN  ELATE  MOLE
OLEG  DINAR  ENID
```

Answer 4

```
JOBS  OKRAS  REAP
ATAT  PEELE  ELLA
WIRETAPPER   PLEA
SCENARIO   ABASER
   OCT   APOS
   SASK  EMPHASISE
RILEY  LAPIS   RMS
ODED  HAREM   AVAS
TEN  MANIA   TRICE
ADENOIDAL   RANK
   ERRS   PIC
ENBLOC  APOTHEGM
MAES  UNFRIENDED
THRO  TIRES  INNS
SAIN  SLOPE  DATE
```

Answer 5

J	I	F	F	■	E	P	I	S	C	■	V	I	A	L
I	D	E	A	■	S	O	N	I	A	■	E	R	I	E
G	E	R	I	A	T	R	I	C	S	■	N	E	R	O
S	E	N	T	I	E	N	T	■	H	I	D	D	E	N
■	■	H	R	S	■	B	E	B	E	■	■	■	■	■
■	R	I	F	E	■	O	B	E	D	I	E	N	C	E
B	O	G	U	S	■	V	A	L	I	D	■	O	L	D
P	U	L	L	■	B	E	N	I	N	■	H	O	E	D
O	T	O	■	M	O	R	T	E	■	T	O	K	A	Y
E	S	O	P	H	A	G	U	S	■	A	S	S	N	■
■	■	S	O	S	O	■	U	M	P	■	■	■	■	■
E	N	C	Y	S	T	■	E	A	R	P	I	E	C	E
M	A	R	C	■	F	U	M	I	G	A	T	I	O	N
U	T	A	H	■	U	D	I	N	E	■	A	R	C	O
S	O	M	E	■	L	O	T	U	S	■	L	E	A	S

Answer 6

B	O	U	T	■	V	E	E	R	S	■	S	C	A	T
R	I	S	E	■	I	G	L	O	O	■	E	L	B	E
A	S	T	R	O	N	O	M	I	C	■	N	O	I	R
N	E	A	T	N	E	S	S	■	I	B	I	D	E	M
■	■	I	L	S	■	T	A	R	O	■	■	■	■	■
■	N	C	A	A	■	B	A	R	B	A	R	I	A	N
G	A	R	R	Y	■	A	D	E	L	E	■	B	R	A
O	K	A	Y	■	B	R	I	B	E	■	L	I	L	I
B	E	N	■	A	R	E	E	L	■	H	A	Z	E	L
I	D	E	O	L	O	G	U	E	■	O	N	A	N	■
■	■	A	L	A	E	■	E	N	D	■	■	■	■	■
T	E	T	R	A	D	■	S	O	D	O	M	I	T	E
E	L	H	I	■	W	A	I	N	W	R	I	G	H	T
A	K	I	N	■	A	B	A	C	I	■	N	O	U	N
K	O	N	G	■	Y	E	M	E	N	■	E	R	D	A

Answer 7

C	A	N	S	■	T	Y	P	A	L	■	B	I	L	E
R	U	I	N	■	H	A	L	L	O	■	U	N	I	S
U	R	B	A	N	O	L	O	G	Y	■	C	C	C	P
E	A	S	T	E	R	L	Y	■	A	A	C	H	E	N
■	■	C	A	N	■	I	L	I	A	■	■	■	■	■
■	R	U	H	R	■	C	A	P	I	L	L	A	R	Y
R	O	B	E	S	■	A	M	E	S	S	■	C	I	E
H	O	O	D	■	E	P	A	C	T	■	P	H	Y	S
E	T	A	■	A	N	I	T	A	■	S	H	O	A	T
A	S	T	H	M	A	T	I	C	■	P	O	O	L	■
■	■	A	B	B	A	■	L	A	N	■	■	■	■	■
C	A	R	R	O	L	■	E	V	E	N	E	D	U	P
W	H	O	A	■	I	N	C	O	N	S	T	A	N	T
T	A	O	S	■	N	O	T	I	N	■	I	N	C	A
S	S	T	S	■	G	R	O	D	Y	■	C	E	O	S

Answer 8

S	A	N	S	■	A	R	R	A	S	■	P	I	T	S
N	A	A	N	■	N	E	E	D	Y	■	E	S	A	U
O	R	N	A	M	E	N	T	A	L	■	A	B	L	E
W	E	A	K	E	N	E	D	■	L	E	R	N	E	R
■	■	E	S	T	■	T	A	E	L	■	■	■	■	■
■	E	X	P	O	■	P	R	O	B	O	S	C	I	S
A	G	A	I	N	■	R	E	L	I	C	■	O	D	A
R	E	C	T	■	M	E	D	I	C	■	A	B	E	T
C	S	T	■	D	E	C	A	F	■	M	C	R	A	E
A	T	O	N	E	T	I	M	E	■	I	C	A	L	■
■	■	E	R	R	S	■	A	L	E	■	■	■	■	■
S	U	R	I	M	I	■	E	U	R	A	S	I	A	N
O	R	I	G	■	C	O	M	P	E	N	S	A	T	E
P	I	T	H	■	A	S	I	A	N	■	E	G	I	S
S	S	T	S	■	L	O	T	T	A	■	D	O	T	S

Answer 9

P	O	D	S		V	E	R	D	I		B	A	I	L
U	H	U	H		A	G	I	S	T		E	U	R	O
R	E	C	E	P	T	A	C	L	E		T	R	O	N
A	D	E	L	A	I	D	E		R	E	H	A	N	G
		T	L	C		H	A	V	E					
	A	P	E	S		P	L	A	T	E	L	I	K	E
K	E	R	R	Y		R	I	V	E	N		A	I	L
O	T	O	S		M	O	K	E	S		A	M	T	S
N	N	W		B	O	W	E	R		A	L	B	E	E
G	A	L	A	T	I	A	N	S		H	E	S	S	
		R	U	E	R			O	O	H				
R	A	W	E	S	T		E	M	P	L	O	Y	E	E
A	D	I	N		I	N	T	H	E	D	U	M	P	S
J	A	N	A		E	A	T	O	N		S	C	O	T
A	M	E	S		S	E	U	S	S		E	A	S	E

Answer 10

T	R	I	A	L		D	U	O	M	O		T	A	L
I	A	M	B	I		U	N	M	A	N		U	B	I
V	I	R	I	D	E	S	C	E	N	T		R	O	N
O	N	E	D		E	T	A	G	E		S	N	U	G
		E	A	R	P		A	G	I	T	A	T	O	
W	I	L	D	F	I	R	E		E	W	E	R		
A	D	O		L	E	O	N	A		O	T	O	E	S
R	E	N	A		R	O	S	S	I		S	U	L	A
M	A	G	D	A		F	O	S	S	E		N	H	L
		H	E	R	B		R	I	S	K	E	D	I	T
F	L	E	A	B	A	G		S	U	E	T			
R	E	A	L		T	R	I	T	E		O	U	R	S
Y	O	D		R	E	A	R	A	D	M	I	R	A	L
E	N	E		E	A	T	E	N		O	L	D	E	R
R	E	D		G	U	E	S	T		S	E	U	S	S

Answer 11

S	H	R	U	B		O	R	C	A	S		C	C	S
G	A	U	N	T		D	O	L	M	A		E	L	L
T	R	I	B	U	L	A	T	I	O	N		N	O	I
S	A	N	O		O	L	I	V	E		S	T	U	D
		L	O	C	I		E	B	B	T	I	D	E	
M	I	S	T	R	U	S	T		A	R	U	M		
E	S	P		E	S	Q	U	E		O	M	E	N	S
A	L	E	F		T	U	R	N	S		P	T	A	H
D	E	C	A	L		E	I	D	E	R		E	P	A
		T	U	T	U		N	U	R	T	U	R	E	D
G	R	A	N	D	P	A		R	A	S	P			
S	E	C	S		S	T	R	A	P		R	H	E	A
T	A	L		D	I	S	O	B	E	D	I	E	N	T
A	T	E		A	D	E	A	L		T	S	L	O	T
R	A	D		D	E	A	R	E		S	E	L	L	S

Answer 12

B	L	O	C	K		P	A	P	U	A		H	A	O
I	O	D	O	L		A	M	A	N	A		E	L	F
A	L	A	R	M	C	L	O	C	K	S		A	G	O
S	A	S	E		O	A	K	E	N		O	R	A	L
		R	U	N	T		D	O	N	A	T	E	D	
M	A	R	S	H	G	A	S		T	A	R	T		
I	L	E		S	O	B	E	R		T	E	H	E	E
C	E	C	E		U	L	C	E	R		D	R	A	T
A	X	E	L	S		E	T	S	E	Q		O	R	T
		S	C	A	B		S	A	T	I	A	B	L	E
R	E	S	I	D	E	S		L	A	D	D			
A	M	I	D		M	A	S	A	I		D	E	M	O
T	O	O		C	O	L	D	B	L	O	O	D	E	D
E	R	N		B	A	S	A	L		U	N	D	I	D
L	Y	S		S	N	A	K	E		T	S	A	R	S

155

Answer 13

I	F	N	O	T		C	A	P	R	A		D	A	O
C	R	A	B	S		O	R	E	A	D		E	S	C
B	A	L	L	E	T	O	M	A	N	E		D	A	T
M	P	A	A		E	P	A	C	T		E	I	N	E
		T	U	N	E		H	E	L	L	C	A	T	
A	L	O	E	V	E	R	A		D	U	M	A		
T	A	S		A	T	A	L	L		C	O	T	A	N
A	S	T	A		S	T	A	I	N		S	O	L	E
T	H	E	M	A		E	N	N	U	I		R	A	N
		N	U	M	B		A	E	R	O	D	Y	N	E
M	I	S	S	T	E	P		A	S	C	H			
A	L	I	E		H	A	U	T	E		A	M	I	S
R	E	B		C	O	N	S	I	D	E	R	A	T	E
E	N	L		P	L	A	T	O		S	M	A	Z	E
S	E	E		A	D	M	A	N		L	A	M	A	R

Answer 14

A	S	P	C	A		T	I	A	R	A		H	T	S
A	C	E	R	B		A	R	B	O	R		E	E	L
H	A	R	U	M	S	C	A	R	U	M		A	P	U
S	G	T	S		A	T	E	A	T		C	R	E	E
		T	I	T	I		M	E	R	I	T	E	D	
E	K	I	S	T	I	C	S		D	R	A	B		
M	O	S		E	N	I	A	C		S	O	R	E	L
E	L	E	A		G	A	H	A	N		S	E	L	A
R	A	N	U	P		N	I	S	U	S		A	H	I
		T	R	A	C		B	U	C	K	S	K	I	N
P	I	R	A	N	H	A		I	L	I	A			
I	D	O	L		A	B	A	S	E		T	B	A	R
L	O	P		E	L	A	S	T	I	C	A	L	L	Y
E	L	I		R	E	C	T	I		S	N	A	K	E
D	S	C		S	T	O	I	C		A	G	H	A	S

Answer 15

B	I	F	I	D		F	O	A	M	S		C	A	B
P	R	I	M	O		A	P	N	E	A		O	M	A
O	I	L	P	A	I	N	T	I	N	G		M	A	S
E	S	M	E		N	A	O	M	I		S	P	I	T
		D	I	E	T		A	A	M	I	L	N	E	
F	O	R	E	N	S	I	C		L	U	N	A		
O	L	E		O	S	C	A	R		G	E	C	K	O
R	E	T	D		E	A	S	E	D		S	E	A	N
T	A	R	A	S		L	E	T	A	T		N	M	E
		A	L	D	A		D	A	R	K	S	T	A	R
R	E	C	L	I	M	B		I	N	O	N			
A	R	T	Y		B	L	I	N	I		O	K	L	A
I	N	I		P	L	A	N	E	T	A	R	I	U	M
L	E	V		A	E	S	I	R		T	E	N	T	Y
S	S	E		O	D	E	T	S		E	D	S	E	L

Answer 16

S	O	P	U	P		S	A	F	E	R		T	L	C
C	H	I	N	A		E	N	A	C	T		H	E	R
A	N	E	S	T	H	E	T	I	Z	E		E	M	I
G	O	R	E		E	D	I	L	E		C	O	M	E
		A	B	R	I		S	M	E	L	L	E	D	
E	F	F	L	U	E	N	T		A	R	E	O		
L	I	A		S	T	E	A	D		R	A	G	A	S
K	E	R	N		O	S	C	A	R		T	I	N	Y
O	F	F	E	D		S	E	V	E	R		A	N	N
		E	R	I	C		T	E	C	T	O	N	I	C
O	U	T	O	F	I	T		N	A	S	A			
A	B	C	S		C	H	I	P	S		K	A	N	E
S	O	H		T	E	E	T	O	T	A	L	L	E	R
T	A	E		O	R	D	E	R		F	E	A	R	S
S	T	D		R	O	A	S	T		L	Y	N	D	E

Answer 17

```
F L I E S ■ S H O A L ■ B U G
A U D I E ■ A A L T O ■ E L I
I N A D V E R T E N T ■ A N S
L E S E ■ A C H O O ■ S C A T
■ ■ R O S A ■ S O O T H E S ■
M E S S I E S T ■ N A I F ■
A M T ■ L I T E R ■ F E R A L
L E A D ■ N I N O N ■ S O M E
A R L E S ■ C E L I A ■ N E V
■ A C L U ■ T E N A N T R Y
E S C A R P S ■ M E S A ■
D U T Y ■ H E L O T ■ S E G A
U P I ■ A E R O D Y N A M I C
C E T ■ C R A T E ■ O L I V E
T R E ■ C E C I L ■ I S L E S
```

Answer 18

```
O A K U M ■ M E A D E ■ H O N
C R A N E ■ A N N E X ■ O S A
T A R R A D I D D L E ■ R I N
O B O E ■ U N S E R ■ A S E A
■ ■ A P E R ■ S I M P E R S ■
C A L L A L O O ■ O R E O ■
O N A ■ S L A B S ■ S A P I D
N I B S ■ O D I U M ■ K E R R
G L O O M ■ S E G A L ■ R O E
■ R O M P ■ S A R A B A N D
A M A T E U R ■ R O M E ■
O A T H ■ R O C C O ■ N O D I
R H O ■ A F G H A N I S T A N
T A R ■ C L E A N ■ L O I N S
A L Y ■ T E R R E ■ O N S E T
```

Answer 19

```
T I R E D ■ C L O A K ■ I B M
O M A N I ■ A I O L I ■ L A I
P A R T N E R S H I P ■ L S D
E M E R ■ O B I E S ■ O U R S
■ A L S O ■ D O O R M A T
E N D P O I N T ■ N O R I ■
P E I ■ S N A C K ■ F I N A L
P O S E ■ S T E I N ■ N A M E
S N U B S ■ E L L I S ■ T B A
■ N O T E ■ L O C U T I O N
S H I N D I G ■ H E B E ■
C O T Y ■ S E L E S ■ D E L E
A R I ■ E N T E R T A I N E D
R A N ■ G E T A T ■ R U N O N
S E G ■ G R O S Z ■ A M A N A
```

Answer 20

```
A R O S E ■ K U D U ■ B O O B
G O D E L ■ O P E N ■ A R L O
N O O N E ■ N A B S ■ A C E R
I M M I G R A T I O N ■ H U N
■ L I U ■ T R I R E M E ■
L I N E S M A N ■ E N E S ■
E S A ■ T E E U P ■ E S T A S
N A T E ■ N O D A L ■ T R A C
O K A P I ■ N E T T S ■ A R A
■ T I C S ■ R E C A L L E D
C L O S E T O ■ O N O ■
L E R ■ R E D U P L I C A T E
E R I C ■ R E N T ■ B A L S A
F O U L ■ N O T A ■ E L G A R
T I M E ■ E N O S ■ L E A R N
```

Answer 21

Answer 22

Answer 23

Answer 24

Answer 25

Answer 26

Answer 27

Answer 28

Answer 29

S	I	T	A	R	■	C	O	R	A	■	L	P	G	A
A	V	I	L	A	■	E	B	A	N	■	C	A	H	N
M	A	N	O	N	■	L	O	B	O	■	D	R	A	T
E	N	T	H	R	A	L	L	I	N	G	■	A	L	I
■	■	■	A	I	R	■	D	Y	N	A	M	I	C	■
E	P	I	S	O	D	E	S	■	M	A	T	A	■	■
M	E	S	■	T	E	L	L	A	■	T	I	R	O	S
E	N	O	L	■	N	O	E	L	S	■	P	I	L	E
R	A	C	E	S	■	N	E	A	L	E	■	B	A	R
■	■	H	E	A	D	■	K	N	O	C	K	O	F	F
T	A	R	R	I	E	D	■	■	S	H	E	■	■	■
I	N	O	■	L	E	A	S	E	H	O	L	D	E	R
A	N	N	I	■	M	R	I	S	■	I	V	A	N	A
R	E	A	L	■	E	L	L	S	■	N	I	N	T	H
A	X	L	E	■	D	A	D	E	■	G	N	A	R	S

Answer 30

H	O	S	E	D	■	A	H	A	S	■	■	P	I	C
O	W	N	E	R	■	N	I	P	A	■	R	E	S	H
M	E	A	N	I	N	G	F	U	L	■	E	R	L	E
E	N	G	■	B	A	R	I	■	A	R	A	F	A	T
■	■	■	A	B	B	Y	■	C	R	E	D	O	■	■
E	M	A	I	L	S	■	L	O	I	T	E	R	E	D
B	A	R	R	E	■	L	A	V	E	D	■	A	D	A
B	Y	E	S	■	R	A	P	E	D	■	A	T	I	T
E	O	N	■	T	A	M	P	S	■	A	B	E	L	E
D	R	A	C	H	M	A	S	■	H	E	A	D	E	D
■	■	C	U	R	B	S	■	M	O	O	D	■	■	■
S	T	E	R	O	L	■	B	O	S	N	■	H	A	D
L	E	O	I	■	I	N	A	P	T	I	T	U	D	E
E	C	U	A	■	N	I	K	E	■	A	E	G	I	S
D	H	S	■	■	G	A	U	D	■	N	A	O	M	I

Answer 31

H	E	D	D	A	■	B	A	A	S	■	■	T	H	O
O	R	S	O	N	■	A	P	P	L	■	A	H	A	B
S	M	O	O	T	H	B	O	R	E	■	C	E	N	O
S	A	S	■	L	O	A	D	■	E	M	E	R	G	E
■	■	E	E	K	S	■	O	P	E	R	E	■	■	■
A	B	L	A	R	E	■	L	A	I	D	B	A	C	K
A	L	E	C	S	■	C	O	K	E	S	■	B	A	R
L	A	S	H	■	S	L	I	E	R	■	B	O	N	O
T	D	S	■	A	C	O	R	N	■	B	R	U	I	N
O	E	I	L	L	A	D	E	■	P	L	A	T	T	E
■	■	S	E	A	L	S	■	D	U	E	T	■	■	■
D	A	M	N	E	D	■	E	A	R	N	■	C	A	L
I	K	O	N	■	I	N	G	R	E	D	I	E	N	T
A	I	R	Y	■	N	A	A	N	■	E	B	B	E	D
N	N	E	■	■	G	E	L	S	■	R	O	U	T	S

Answer 32

A	L	L	A	N	■	A	B	A	T	■	■	A	M	O
L	O	U	P	E	■	D	E	L	A	■	A	M	I	D
L	U	B	R	I	C	A	T	E	S	■	M	A	C	E
A	D	E	■	T	A	P	A	■	K	E	E	L	E	D
■	■	■	S	H	U	T	■	A	W	I	N	G	■	■
G	R	E	T	E	L	■	O	N	O	N	D	A	G	A
E	A	G	E	R	■	C	A	D	R	E	■	M	E	D
A	V	O	W	■	B	A	T	I	K	■	R	A	S	A
R	E	C	■	S	A	R	E	E	■	P	A	T	T	I
S	L	E	E	P	E	R	S	■	C	A	R	E	E	R
■	■	N	E	E	D	Y	■	D	U	L	E	■	■	■
A	T	T	L	E	E	■	O	U	R	S	■	S	I	E
B	A	R	E	■	K	I	N	D	L	I	N	E	S	S
I	B	I	D	■	E	S	T	E	■	E	U	R	O	S
E	S	C	■	■	R	H	O	S	■	D	I	A	N	E

Answer 33

Answer 34

Answer 35

Answer 36

Answer 37

L	I	A	N	E		A	S	I	S				C	S	A
I	N	L	A	Y		E	L	S	A		O	H	E	D	
C	O	M	M	E	N	T	A	R	Y		B	A	R	E	
E	N	A		L	A	N	G		O	D	E	N	S	E	
		H	A	N	A		S	N	E	A	D				
A	R	I	O	S	O		P	O	A	C	H	E	R	S	
T	E	N	C	H		H	E	N	R	I		L	O	A	
H	U	N	K		M	E	N	S	A		P	I	K	E	
O	S	O		F	A	N	N	Y		G	R	E	E	N	
S	E	M	O	L	I	N	A		C	H	I	R	R	S	
		I	R	O	N	Y		A	P	E	X				
C	A	N	O	E	S		M	C	A	T		B	I	S	
O	M	A	N		T	H	I	R	S	T	I	E	S	T	
D	O	T	O		E	R	L	E		O	G	L	E	D	
A	Y	E			M	E	L	D		S	O	L	E	S	

Answer 38

R	A	P	E	D		S	N	A	G			E	T	C	
O	V	A	T	E		K	O	L	A		E	T	A	L	
O	O	P	H	O	R	I	T	I	S		N	E	M	O	
D	N	A		R	I	T	A		P	A	I	R	E	D	
		R	B	I	S		R	E	M	A	N				
M	A	Q	U	I	S		D	E	D	U	C	I	N	G	
C	O	U	N	T		S	O	L	A	R		T	E	L	
G	R	A	S		L	O	Y	A	L		D	I	V	A	
E	T	D		T	E	L	E	X		T	H	E	I	R	
E	A	R	T	H	M	A	N		C	H	A	S	S	E	
		A	A	R	O	N		N	A	I	L				
C	A	N	N	O	N		B	U	R	T		A	D	A	
R	I	G	G		A	N	A	L	P	H	A	B	E	T	
A	R	L	O		D	A	H	L		E	L	E	C	T	
B	Y	E			E	S	T	S		R	A	D	O	N	

Answer 39

F	L	A	K	E		M	O	I	L			G	E	R	I
I	O	D	I	N		A	L	T	O			E	M	E	R
B	O	U	N	D	A	R	I	E	S			C	E	C	E
S	S	E		E	L	M	O	R	E		K	E	A	N	
		N	A	T	O			T	H	O	R	P	E		
L	A	B	O	R	A	T	O	R	I	E	S				
A	N	T	I	S		K	A	M	A		H	A	H		
C	A	U	L		P	A	R	S	E		N	O	R	A	
E	T	S		B	A	B	A		H	U	N	C	H		
		I	L	L	U	S	T	R	A	T	I	O	N		
D	A	K	O	T	A		B	U	G	S					
E	G	A	D		T	E	E	O	F	F		E	P	A	
L	O	R	I		I	R	O	N	F	I	S	T	E	D	
I	N	E	Z		A	N	N	E		S	A	C	R	A	
S	Y	N	E		L	E	S	S		H	O	H	U	M	

Answer 40

S	C	A	L	L		S	H	O	P		R	E	N	E	
C	U	T	I	E		H	E	I	R		E	C	O	L	
A	B	O	M	I	N	A	B	L	E		G	O	T	O	
D	E	M		S	A	F	E	S	T		G	L	O	P	
		S	T	A	T			E	L	A	I	N	E		
H	A	P	P	E	N	S	T	A	N	C	E				
M	O	L	A	R		A	B	C	D		S	A	G		
O	N	I	T		C	A	N	O	E		G	A	W	P	
S	E	E		R	I	G	G		S	O	L	E	A		
		N	E	C	E	S	S	I	T	A	T	E	S		
H	A	B	I	L	E		A	B	E	T					
A	L	O	P		R	I	B	B	O	N		S	C	I	
C	L	I	P		O	V	E	R	S	T	A	T	E	D	
K	I	T	E		N	A	T	E		O	V	A	R	Y	
S	E	E	R		E	N	E	S		R	E	B	E	L	

Answer 41

S	P	I	R	E		R	O	A	D			S	S	G	T
A	I	R	E	D		E	L	S	E			C	A	R	E
A	N	A	L	G	E	S	I	C	S		H	U	E	D	
B	Y	E		I	R	O	N	I	C		O	D	E	D	
		G	E	O	L		R	A	R	I	T	Y			
N	O	N	E	S	S	E	N	T	I	A	L				
O	R	A	N	T		J	A	B	S		E	E	C		
S	A	B	U		A	B	O	V	E		O	S	L	O	
E	L	S		S	L	U	R			O	R	T	H	O	
		G	U	A	R	D	I	A	N	S	H	I	P		
N	O	R	D	I	C		N	D	A	K					
O	D	E	A		A	B	A	S	E	D		A	L	A	
P	E	N	N		R	E	M	I	N	I	S	C	E	D	
E	S	T	S		T	E	A	T		E	T	A	G	E	
S	A	S	K		E	T	T	U		T	E	R	S	E	

Answer 42

D	E	N	I	S		T	B	S	P		M	I	S	S
A	L	E	C	K		E	Y	E	R		I	D	O	L
M	A	R	I	O	N	E	T	T	E		D	A	L	Y
P	L	O		O	U	T	E	A	T		D	H	A	L
		O	K	I	E		T	H	E	O	R	Y		
M	A	L	N	U	T	R	I	T	I	O	N			
P	S	A	L	M		L	E	F	T		T	A	B	
A	H	O	Y		S	L	I	M	Y		T	H	E	O
A	Y	S		L	U	A	U			L	E	A	R	N
	A	S	S	I	M	I	L	A	T	I	O	N		
E	M	M	E	T	T		N	A	S	H				
M	A	Y	O		A	B	A	C	U	S		A	G	E
B	R	E	L		I	R	R	A	D	I	A	T	E	D
E	C	R	U		N	U	T	S		E	K	I	N	G
D	O	S	S		S	T	Y	E		S	A	T	A	Y

Answer 43

G	O	O	N	S		I	N	S	P		K	A	M	I
O	R	O	N	O		N	A	L	A		E	C	O	N
B	E	N	E	F	A	C	T	O	R		B	E	R	G
I	L	A		A	M	O	E	B	A		A	R	A	L
		A	R	U	M		K	I	B	B	L	E		
P	R	E	P	A	R	E	D	N	E	S	S			
H	O	B	O	S		O	G	E	E		I	R	E	
A	S	A	P		H	E	L	O	T		A	B	E	L
R	E	N		B	A	S	E		S	M	A	C	K	
	H	A	R	P	S	I	C	H	O	R	D	S		
S	E	D	O	N	A		N	O	O	K				
O	P	E	L		K	A	I	S	E	R		M	O	E
D	O	L	L		I	N	T	E	N	T	I	O	N	S
A	C	T	O		R	O	A	R		E	S	S	E	S
S	H	A	W		I	N	S	T		N	O	T	R	E

Answer 44

B	L	A	N	K		O	D	E	A		P	I	N	G
R	O	U	S	E		P	E	R	M		I	S	A	R
I	N	T	A	N	G	I	B	L	E		E	I	N	E
C	E	O		N	E	A	T	E	N		R	A	C	E
		L	E	N	T		A	A	C	H	E	N		
I	R	R	E	D	E	E	M	A	B	L	E			
S	A	U	C	Y		C	A	L	F		B	A	M	
L	U	S	H		A	L	G	A	E		B	O	M	B
A	L	S		E	D	I	E			I	O	N	I	A
	P	R	E	D	E	C	E	S	S	O	R	S		
A	N	N	E	A	L		A	M	O	S				
B	A	E	R		A	R	M	P	I	T		S	E	I
A	G	A	R		I	D	E	O	L	O	G	I	S	T
C	A	T	O		D	A	W	N		P	O	R	T	E
A	T	O	N		E	S	S	E		E	P	E	E	S

Answer 45

B	A	R	E	S	■	S	I	M	P	■	S	A	R	I
A	C	C	R	A	■	N	C	A	R	■	A	D	E	S
R	E	M	A	R	K	A	B	L	E	■	M	D	S	E
A	R	P	■	C	R	I	M	E	S	■	B	E	A	R
■	■	C	O	I	L	■	■	E	C	A	R	T	E	■
C	O	M	M	I	S	S	I	O	N	E	R	■	■	■
O	H	G	O	D	■	L	A	C	E	■	M	A	B	■
L	I	M	N	■	A	L	I	F	E	■	B	I	T	E
D	O	T	■	F	L	E	A	■	■	I	O	D	O	L
■	■	H	A	I	R	D	R	E	S	S	I	N	G	■
D	E	L	U	X	E	■	■	A	L	A	N	■	■	■
R	B	I	S	■	N	E	A	R	E	D	■	I	L	A
E	O	N	S	■	A	N	T	E	M	O	R	T	E	M
A	L	G	A	■	G	O	O	F	■	R	A	S	T	A
D	I	O	R	■	E	S	P	Y	■	A	F	O	O	T

Answer 46

P	A	D	R	E	■	B	L	A	S	■	S	A	S	S
A	N	I	M	A	■	L	O	B	E	■	H	E	E	L
A	N	E	S	T	H	E	S	I	A	■	E	G	G	Y
R	A	D	■	C	O	A	S	T	S	■	E	I	N	E
■	■	C	R	O	C	■	■	C	E	N	S	O	R	■
C	H	E	M	O	T	H	E	R	A	P	Y	■	■	■
B	E	L	O	W	■	C	A	P	A	■	B	B	B	■
E	W	E	N	■	F	A	L	S	E	■	H	A	R	A
R	N	A	■	L	E	N	A	■	■	C	E	S	A	R
■	■	F	A	I	N	T	H	E	A	R	T	E	D	■
P	E	G	L	E	G	■	■	A	R	L	O	■	■	■
O	B	O	E	■	N	I	H	I	L	O	■	K	A	I
D	O	U	X	■	I	T	I	N	E	R	A	N	T	S
I	N	G	E	■	N	A	D	A	■	I	R	A	T	E
A	Y	E	S	■	G	L	E	N	■	C	A	R	N	E

Answer 47

A	G	O	R	A	■	H	A	R	P	■	M	A	A	S
S	E	C	T	S	■	O	D	O	R	■	I	F	S	O
C	R	A	S	S	I	T	U	D	E	■	N	O	O	N
H	E	S	■	E	S	T	E	E	M	■	C	O	N	Y
■	■	E	R	L	E	■	■	I	C	E	T	E	A	■
C	H	E	S	T	E	R	F	I	E	L	D	■	■	■
H	A	L	T	S	■	O	G	R	E	■	B	B	C	■
E	N	I	D	■	C	H	L	O	E	■	B	O	A	T
F	A	A	■	C	O	E	D	■	■	C	L	O	W	N
■	■	H	A	R	P	S	I	C	H	O	R	D	S	■
S	H	I	E	L	D	■	■	S	L	A	B	■	■	■
H	A	R	I	■	L	A	B	O	U	R	■	J	O	S
A	V	A	S	■	E	N	A	M	E	L	L	I	N	G
C	E	N	T	■	S	A	B	E	■	E	S	B	A	T
K	R	I	S	■	S	T	A	R	■	S	T	E	N	S

Answer 48

S	I	A	M	■	M	A	R	L	A	■	C	P	A	S
O	N	D	E	■	O	S	I	E	R	■	L	A	G	O
I	D	E	A	L	I	S	T	I	C	■	O	C	A	S
E	Y	E	T	O	E	Y	E	■	H	E	T	E	R	O
■	■	■	L	T	R	■	A	N	K	H	S	■	■	■
D	E	A	D	L	Y	■	S	K	E	E	■	E	G	G
E	N	N	I	S	■	S	H	E	S	■	A	T	O	N
A	S	E	A	■	F	O	O	L	S	■	A	T	T	A
R	U	M	S	■	A	B	R	A	■	G	R	E	A	T
E	E	O	■	I	M	I	T	■	A	L	E	R	T	S
■	■	M	R	B	I	G	■	C	P	O	■	■	■	■
O	C	E	A	N	S	■	A	E	R	O	B	I	C	S
A	R	T	I	■	H	E	B	D	O	M	A	D	A	L
R	U	E	D	■	E	L	I	A	N	■	N	E	M	O
S	E	R	S	■	D	O	E	R	S	■	G	A	P	E

164

Answer 49

C	O	N	S	■	R	A	G	A	S	■	A	F	A	R
L	O	A	M	■	E	D	U	C	E	■	B	A	L	E
I	N	S	U	R	G	E	N	C	E	■	A	T	O	P
P	A	T	T	E	R	N	S	■	M	A	C	A	W	S
■	■	N	E	O	■	L	T	C	O	L	■	■	■	■
G	O	E	S	A	T	■	O	H	O	S	■	I	N	S
A	V	A	I	L	■	A	R	A	B	■	A	S	I	A
B	O	R	N	■	C	U	R	S	E	■	I	T	E	R
L	I	T	E	■	A	R	I	A	■	C	L	I	C	K
E	D	H	■	R	B	I	S	■	P	I	S	C	E	S
■	I	L	I	A	C	■	M	O	A	■	■	■	■	■
M	A	N	U	A	L	■	M	E	M	O	R	I	E	S
E	M	E	R	■	I	N	O	N	E	S	E	N	S	E
R	I	S	E	■	S	M	A	L	L	■	A	T	M	S
C	E	S	S	■	M	E	T	O	O	■	M	I	E	S

Answer 50

M	A	C	E	■	B	E	E	R	S	■	C	P	A	S
B	U	R	S	■	A	A	R	O	N	■	H	E	L	I
A	D	A	M	A	N	T	I	N	E	■	I	R	O	N
S	I	B	E	L	I	U	S	■	A	I	R	M	E	N
■	■	■	A	S	P	■	O	K	A	P	I	■	■	■
D	A	L	E	T	H	■	L	O	I	N	■	S	H	A
A	D	E	L	E	■	F	A	Z	E	■	I	S	I	N
C	E	P	E	■	C	O	V	E	R	■	K	I	L	T
C	A	R	A	■	A	C	A	D	■	G	E	O	D	E
A	L	E	■	E	R	A	S	■	L	I	A	N	A	S
■	C	R	E	E	L	■	E	E	L	■	■	■	■	■
A	S	H	O	R	E	■	S	C	A	L	L	I	O	N
P	E	A	U	■	N	O	N	O	N	S	E	N	S	E
P	L	U	G	■	E	D	I	L	E	■	A	G	H	A
S	A	N	E	■	D	A	T	E	D	■	D	E	A	L

Answer 51

S	A	A	B	■	C	O	I	L	S	■	S	M	E	E
K	E	P	I	■	A	N	N	I	E	■	H	O	L	A
I	R	O	N	F	I	S	T	E	D	■	A	N	E	T
D	O	D	D	E	R	E	R	■	A	O	R	T	A	S
■	■	■	A	N	T	■	A	T	R	I	P	■	■	■
C	O	L	O	R	S	■	A	V	I	D	■	E	A	P
A	M	O	R	S	■	O	L	A	V	■	A	L	L	A
R	A	V	E	■	A	L	E	N	E	■	D	I	O	S
E	N	E	S	■	N	E	U	T	■	K	E	E	N	E
S	I	P	■	A	T	I	T	■	O	V	E	R	G	O
■	O	S	R	I	C	■	M	B	A	■	■	■	■	■
S	A	T	I	N	G	■	G	O	S	S	A	M	E	R
A	R	I	Z	■	O	P	P	R	E	S	S	I	V	E
F	L	O	E	■	N	E	A	T	S	■	C	R	A	M
E	O	N	S	■	E	A	S	E	S	■	H	A	N	S

Answer 52

B	E	R	M	■	S	C	E	N	A	■	C	E	C	E
D	D	A	Y	■	C	A	R	O	L	■	A	T	A	T
R	I	P	R	O	A	R	I	N	G	■	C	E	L	T
M	E	T	A	L	L	I	C	■	I	C	A	R	I	A
■	■	■	■	L	A	B	■	A	C	T	O	N	■	■
A	F	F	A	I	R	■	K	R	I	S	■	I	R	R
G	L	A	R	E	■	H	E	A	D	■	P	T	A	H
R	A	L	E	■	M	A	Y	B	E	■	A	I	R	E
I	M	S	O	■	E	L	I	S	■	F	L	E	E	T
N	E	E	■	A	T	T	N	■	P	R	E	S	E	T
■	H	E	R	E	S	■	A	A	A	■	■	■	■	■
O	D	O	N	T	O	■	A	L	L	I	A	N	C	E
L	E	O	I	■	R	A	D	I	A	L	T	I	R	E
A	L	D	A	■	I	D	E	S	T	■	O	N	E	G
F	I	S	C	■	C	A	S	T	E	■	M	A	W	S

Answer 53

```
N C A A   S A M O S   S I S I
A L B A   I M I D E   A N A T
B A R R A M U N D A   N A T E
S N A P P I S H   R E D D E R
      O L E   C O P S E
I N H E R E   J A V A   Q E D
R I A N T   F A T E   F U S E
A G R O   N I C E R   R A T E
N E D S   O A K S   D E C O R
I L K   I N T O   R E T Y P E
    N I S U S   H E S
R O O S T S   N E C K L A C E
O R C S   E N C L O S U R E S
B A K U   R E A I R   R E S T
E L S E   S C R O D   K A T E
```

Answer 54

```
R A B E   G H A N A   B R I E
B I E N   L A D E D   E E L S
I R R E S O L U T E   A S S T
S E N S I B L E   Q A N T A S
  R A E   F U R O R
D A N I E L   M A A M   I A N
A W A R D   L A I C   A C N E
D A N A   F A I R Y   L T D S
A R O N   R P M S   E B E R T
S E S   R U E S   B L A D E S
  E M A I L   G A L
D E C E I T   S E S A M O I D
E N O S   A C C E S S I B L E
C O N N   G O O S E   L E I A
O L D E   E S T E S   E Y E D
```

Answer 55

```
N D A K   N I E L S   O F F S
A R C A   I O D I C   C O L A
R E T R A C T I L E   E R I K
K E E L B O A T   P L A T T E
  I L S   A T O N Y
B L O N D E   L I R A   N O N
A L B E E   B A L E   L I M E
S A L A   G A T E S   A N E W
I M I T   O K E Y   A N E N T
L A G   I B E X   E V E R S O
  A I R E R   B A A
J I T N E Y   A R G I N I N E
A T I T   O S C I L L A T E D
D I O R   N I E C E   N A V E
E N N A   D E S K S   A L A N
```

Answer 56

```
H I C K   C H E E K   C P O S
I D L Y   H O W S O   A L V A
N E E R D O W E L L   L E A K
D E F A U L T S   I D E A L S
  C E O   K N O B S
S A M B A R   R E S H   A S H
C R E E L   M A R K   P N E U
A L A N   C A B B Y   I T E R
L E N D   A C I S   P O R T O
E N D   A B A D   C A N Y O N
  E N D O W   A R T
R E R O O T   I N A T R I C E
A M I R   A D D I T I O N A L
P E N N   G A Y L E   B R I M
E R G S   E L L E R   B E N S
```

Answer 57

Answer 58

Answer 59

Answer 60

Answer 61

```
C A R E ■ A B A S E ■ F O R K
L U I S ■ C O N A N ■ A B U T
A D A K ■ I T E M S ■ L O S S
P I T I E D ■ L O O K S E E ■
S E A M S ■ E A R L E ■
■ O T O S ■ E T H A N
D A M ■ O N E M O R E T I M E
E L E A ■ A R A C E ■ O L I O
C A R D I N A L A T E ■ O E N
O I L E D ■ S D A K ■
■ L Y R I C ■ R I C A N
■ R E A L I S E ■ O P T I M A
L O T I ■ N O R A D ■ B L A S
E S T D ■ G L E B E ■ A I D A
I S E E ■ O A S E S ■ G A O L
```

Answer 62

```
H O D S ■ L A M I A ■ L A G O
E P E E ■ A B Y S S ■ I C O N
M E W L ■ B U R S T ■ M H O S
P R E E N S ■ R E I G N E D ■
S A Y N O ■ H I R E E ■
■ A A R P ■ O T E R O
F A S ■ H O R O L O G I C A L
I D E A ■ A E S I R ■ C O K E
F O R B I D D A N C E ■ L E S
E S S E N ■ A H A B ■
■ D A N C E ■ S A N A A
■ L I N S E E D ■ A T T E N D
D Y K E ■ A L E P H ■ H A N D
O L E G ■ L I N G O ■ E L A L
M E S O ■ S A S S Y ■ R E N E
```

Answer 63

```
R A B E ■ M I C A H ■ E M I L
A B E D ■ A T O M Y ■ D A D A
B A R I ■ N O R M A ■ G W E N
I C E T E A ■ G A T H E R S ■
D A T E R ■ I N T O W ■
■ D O B S ■ P I L E S
D O E ■ S O C I A L I S T I C
I K E A ■ R A N T O ■ E D N A
P R O B L E M A T I C ■ S E G
S A C R E ■ S N I G ■
■ A E S O P ■ S N A P S
■ C O S T A T E ■ A T O M I C
L A N I ■ B E T A S ■ M I S O
A V I V ■ I R A N I ■ O T T O
M E T E ■ N O L A N ■ N Y E T
```

Answer 64

```
P E P S ■ S I G M A ■ D R A G
A Y A H ■ C L U E D ■ O O N A
B R R R ■ A S I D E ■ N O A M
L I K I N G ■ S A L A A M S ■
O R A L E ■ E L E C T ■
■ L U B E ■ A I D A N
M B A ■ R E I N C A R N A T E
L O R D ■ A N I O N ■ G R I T
L A B I O D E N T A L ■ N T H
E S S A Y ■ E T O N ■
■ M E R E S ■ G O A L S
■ E M E R I T A ■ S E R G E I
A M A T ■ C A R L A ■ M A M E
I M R E ■ E G A D S ■ A T O N
D E E R ■ D E N S E ■ L E N A
```

Answer 65

Answer 66

Answer 67

Answer 68

169

Answer 69

```
D A C C A ■ A K I R A ■ E R B
I S L A M ■ E A T E N ■ S A E
C H A M B E R L A I N ■ P P S
K E N ■ A M I E ■ G U I L T S
■ ■ A G U E ■ J N A N A ■ ■
S E D G E S ■ C E I L I N G S
A P E R S ■ G R A N S ■ A L E
B O L O ■ P R O N G ■ O D I E
E D E ■ B R E N S ■ O N E N D
R E G A L I T Y ■ C R E S T S
■ ■ A R O M A ■ P A D S ■ ■
M E T E O R ■ P U L I ■ L P S
O N I ■ D O C T R I N A I R E
O D O ■ E S T E S ■ A I M E E
R E N ■ D E R R Y ■ L L O Y D
```

Answer 70

```
C L A C K ■ M E A D E ■ O N A
E Y D I E ■ A D M A N ■ P A R
R E A R R A N G I N G ■ E M I
E S S ■ N I L E ■ D R O N E D
■ ■ H E D Y ■ B R O O M ■ ■
A N G O L A ■ B L U S H I N G
G I L A S ■ C L E F S ■ N E A
G N A R ■ C H I E F ■ E D A M
I O S ■ N O E N D ■ A D E L E
E N S L A V E D ■ P R I D E S
■ ■ H A V E R ■ P E R E ■ ■
L O O K A T ■ K A N A ■ K O A
E A U ■ R O M A N T I C I S M
A H S ■ R U S K S ■ G E E S E
D U E ■ E S S A Y ■ N O V A S
```

Answer 71

```
Q A N D A ■ O K A P I ■ R F D
A P A R T ■ R E R A N ■ E L Y
D O V E T A I L I N G ■ M A E
I C Y ■ A P O P ■ B R O O M S
■ ■ L I O N ■ B R A I D ■ ■
C H A I N S ■ R O O T L E S S
H U L A S ■ H E N I E ■ L E E
E M I R ■ G I M E L ■ A L G A
C A M ■ A R R A S ■ A L E U T
K N E E D E E P ■ B L A D E S
■ ■ N A M E D ■ H A L S ■ ■
A S T R I D ■ L O U T ■ A G A
R C A ■ R I G O R M O R T I S
M A R ■ A L O U D ■ L I O N S
A M Y ■ L Y N D E ■ D O N A T
```

Answer 72

```
E L L I E ■ E C O L E ■ B E A
K E A T S ■ L A V E R ■ A S L
E I N S T E I N I U M ■ S A O
D A D ■ H A A S ■ K I C K U P
■ ■ H E S S ■ B E N N E ■ ■
S C A T T Y ■ L A M E N T E D
C H U T E ■ P E R I S ■ B R O
R A S P ■ M A G D A ■ B A I T
A S T ■ P A P A S ■ M U L C T
G E R M I N A L ■ O U T L A Y
■ ■ A R N E L ■ A P T S ■ ■
S A L I N A ■ F L E A ■ A D E
C P I ■ A T E L E C T A S I S
A S A ■ C E D A R ■ E X E A T
R E N ■ E R U P T ■ S E A L S
```

Answer 73

P	I	P	E	D	■	E	G	G	A	R	■	S	B	S
O	V	A	T	E	■	B	O	U	S	E	■	C	I	A
L	E	C	H	E	R	O	U	S	L	Y	■	R	N	S
O	S	A	■	P	A	L	P	■	O	N	R	U	S	H
■	■	B	E	T	A	■	E	N	A	C	T	■	■	■
E	L	A	Y	N	E	■	M	I	G	R	A	I	N	E
M	I	L	T	S	■	H	O	D	A	D	■	N	A	V
C	E	P	E	■	D	O	P	E	S	■	M	I	N	E
E	O	E	■	M	I	T	E	R	■	L	A	Z	A	R
E	N	N	O	B	L	E	D	■	D	I	G	E	S	T
■	■	S	C	A	L	L	■	M	O	K	E	■	■	■
G	A	T	S	B	Y	■	K	I	T	E	■	M	O	I
A	M	O	■	A	B	A	N	D	O	N	M	E	N	T
B	I	C	■	N	A	P	E	S	■	E	A	G	L	E
E	E	K	■	E	G	R	E	T	■	D	R	A	Y	S

Answer 74

B	E	M	A	D	■	E	S	S	E	N	■	B	B	B
I	L	E	N	E	■	P	A	E	S	E	■	E	R	R
A	S	S	A	S	S	I	N	A	T	E	■	S	A	E
S	A	S	■	C	A	C	O	■	E	D	I	T	E	D
■	■	■	R	E	B	S	■	C	E	L	L	S	■	■
S	A	L	I	N	E	■	C	A	M	E	L	E	E	R
E	L	A	N	D	■	F	A	R	E	D	■	L	A	O
D	E	C	K	■	P	I	N	E	D	■	I	L	S	A
E	V	E	■	O	R	B	I	T	■	G	R	E	E	D
R	E	R	E	C	O	R	D	■	G	U	A	R	D	S
■	■	A	G	A	T	E	■	B	U	N	S	■	■	■
A	C	T	O	N	E	■	A	L	L	S	■	E	B	B
J	A	I	■	A	G	O	R	A	P	H	O	B	I	A
A	N	N	■	D	E	P	T	H	■	I	N	A	L	L
R	E	G	■	A	S	S	E	S	■	P	A	N	E	L

Answer 75

C	A	B	A	L	■	O	K	I	E	S	■	P	B	S
A	C	E	T	O	■	R	E	N	T	A	■	A	A	A
R	A	T	T	L	E	B	R	A	I	N	■	I	A	N
E	D	H	■	L	A	I	N	■	O	D	E	N	S	E
■	■	O	A	S	T	■	F	L	A	C	K	■	■	■
M	E	M	O	R	Y	■	M	E	A	L	T	I	M	E
E	L	A	N	D	■	P	O	U	T	S	■	L	I	L
A	L	T	A	■	E	L	U	D	E	■	A	L	L	I
D	E	C	■	A	N	I	L	S	■	P	L	E	N	A
E	N	H	A	N	C	E	D	■	C	A	D	R	E	S
■	■	M	O	O	R	S	■	M	A	L	A	■	■	■
R	I	A	L	T	O	■	C	A	R	A	■	D	O	A
O	R	K	■	H	A	R	U	M	S	C	A	R	U	M
L	E	E	■	E	C	O	L	I	■	E	L	Y	S	E
F	D	R	■	R	H	Y	M	E	■	S	A	S	E	S

Imprint
Tim Rosenbladt
Carissa, Block 14, Flat 7A
Triq F. Vidal, Ibrag
SWQ 2471, Malta

Puzzles are created using Crossword Express